L I F E
MAKEOVERS

ALSO BY CHERYL RICHARDSON

Stand Up for Your Life

Take Time for Your Life

LIFE
MAKEOVERS

52 Practical and Inspiring

Ways to Improve Your Life

One Week at a Time

CHERYL
RICHARDSON

BROADWAY BOOKS   NEW YORK

Broadway Books titles may be purchased for business or promotional use or for special sales. For information, please write to: Special Markets Department, Random House, Inc., 1540 Broadway, New York, NY 10036.

PRINTED IN THE UNITED STATES OF AMERICA

BROADWAY BOOKS and its logo, a letter B bisected on the diagonal, are trademarks of Broadway Books, a division of Random House, Inc.

The Library of Congress has cataloged the hardcover edition as follows:

Richardson, Cheryl.
    Life makeovers : 52 practical and inspiring ways to improve your life one week at a time / Cheryl Richardson. — 1st ed.
        p.   cm.
    Includes bibliographical references.
    1. Conduct of life.   I. Title.
BF637.C5   R52   2000
158.1 — dc21   00-040315

Visit our website at www.broadwaybooks.com

First trade paperback edition published 2002

Designed by Mauna Eichner

ISBN 0-7679-0884-8

10   9   8   7   6   5   4   3   2   1

To my husband Michael,

the man whose presence and love

always return me to center.

ACKNOWLEDGMENTS

When you ask most authors about their publishing experiences, you usually hear stories of frustration or disappointment. Not this author. I have been blessed with an amazing team of men and women at Broadway Books who stand behind me one hundred percent.

My editor Lauren Marino is first in line. Thank you for supporting me in your wise and loving way and for challenging me to craft a "word of mouth" worthy book. My publicist Debbie Stier is an amazing woman. Her skill, enthusiasm, and relentless determination are just a few of the many assets that make her the best in the business. Thank you for believing in me, Debbie, *and* for lining up the stars!

Thanks to Robert Allen for covering all the bases every step of the way and to the rest of the Broadway team: Mario Pulice, Roberto de Vicq de Cumptich, Heather Flaherty, Brian Jones, Cate Tynan, Ruth Hein, and the best sales force in the business!

My agent David Smith, president of DHS Literary, has been an important business partner and friend. Thank you for guiding my publishing career with enthusiasm and integrity. And thank you to my publicist Christina Young, a true professional who took my work to heart and handled my publicity with the utmost care.

As I write these acknowledgments I struggle to find a way to thank each and every one of the dear, dear friends who have played a key role in my success. At the risk of leaving even one person out, let me say to each of you that I can't thank you enough for loving me and for holding the vision of my work, especially on those days when I let go.

I am very lucky to have a large family who love me unconditionally and support my work with a passion—they're a publicity department and sales force in and of themselves. A heartfelt thanks to my mom and dad, and my sisters and brothers Steven, Janice, Donna, Tom, Lisa, Walter, Shelly, Mark, Robert, Karen, Kerri, Missy, and Max, as well as my in-laws Pat and Curt Gerrish.

To my dear friend and coach Shirley Anderson, thank you for your wise counsel and valuable editorial input, especially at the beach! You are my "Yoda." And a very special thanks to Marilyn Abraham, who continues to be my guardian angel from afar.

I am deeply grateful to Thomas Leonard for his introduction to the concept of "extreme self-care," a concept that has changed my life and the lives of so many others. And I'd like to acknowledge my friends and colleagues at Coach University, especially Melinda and Sandy Vilas, CEO of CoachInc.com, for their dedication to a profession that is changing people's lives.

I'd like to thank Katy Murphy Davis for believing in my work and for keeping the idea alive until the time was right, and Andrea Wishom for being such a joy to work with. And my heartfelt thanks to Oprah for changing my life.

My personal assistant Jan Silva is a godsend! Thank you for keeping my life so well organized and for being a calm force during the most hectic of times.

This book was inspired by the thousands of men and women who make up the Life Makeover online community. Every encouraging e-mail, question, and thought-provoking comment has become an important part of these pages. Thank you for your dedication to living an authentic life and making the world a more loving place to be.

My husband Michael Gerrish is a very special man. Without his love, unwavering support, keen intuitive insight, and nonstop comedy routines, I would not be where I am today. I love you, Michael, infinity times infinity.

And finally, I thank God—the Divine force that guides my life.

CONTENTS

INTRODUCTION

How often do you daydream about living a better life — a life that reflects more of *you*, your values and deepest desires? How many times have you come to the end of a busy week and toyed with the fantasy of packing a bag and leaving it all behind? I'm sure I don't need to tell you that in today's world most people live with a nagging sense that something's missing or that life is passing them by. So many of us long for time to discover who we are and what we really want before it's too late.

For the last nine years I've worked as a personal coach helping clients to reevaluate their lives and connect more deeply with what really matters most. The goal was to improve the quality of their lives. The improvements varied, depending on the client. For some, new jobs that honored their values and their need for a life outside of work helped make a difference. For others, getting the right support or putting smart systems in place allowed them to eliminate the stress of success. And, it was not uncommon for clients to scale back or simplify their lives dramatically in order to reclaim the peace and serenity they desired. Each client's story was unique, and yet they all had one common goal — to live a more authentic life, one that reflected their values and most treasured priorities. Let's see if any of these stories sound familiar. . . .

As Olivia stands by the window in her office looking out over the city, she wonders where her life is headed. Working as a manager for a high-tech company, she feels like she's been on a wild ride. Stock prices are up, sales are strong, and she's been a major contributor to the success of her division. Her work used to be rewarding, but now Olivia feels miserable. Although she found the life she thought she wanted, she feels as if she's lost herself.

Olivia gets up early every day, hits the gym by 6, gets to her desk by 8, and on most nights leaves the office after 7:30. She daydreams about how life used to be when she spent more time with her friends, dated on a regular basis, and had more time to herself. At this point Olivia says that her life feels like one long routine day after another. She's tired, lonely, and ready for a change.

Olivia's situation is a good example of what happens when we dedicate so much of our life to work — we end up missing our life. We forge ahead, get many of our needs — such as the need for community, recognition, or accomplishment — met at work, and suddenly discover that we no longer have a personal life to go home to. This realization can be a hard pill to swallow.

Sometimes, however, the problem is a little different. For example, in David's situation, his success has given him much more than he bargained for. Sitting at his desk at the end of a busy day David wonders if all his hard work is really paying off. His consulting business is more successful than ever. He's made more money this year than in the last two years combined. And, he can barely remember the days when he worried about making payroll. Yet David walks around with a nagging feeling that something is missing. Although he's reached the level of success he always hoped for, it doesn't feel the way he expected it to feel. He has more responsibility than ever — a loving wife, three small kids, a large house in the country, and twenty-five employees to manage. Instead of feeling happy about the role he's created for himself, David says he feels like an employee working for everyone else. He often fantasizes about selling the business, downsizing his family's lifestyle, and trying something new. David's not sure he's willing to continue paying such a high price for success.

Or there's Margaret, whose unhappiness has more to do with

an inner challenge than with her external circumstances. After dropping the kids off at school, Margaret drives to work feeling conflicted. The mother of two boys and the owner of a wholesale gift company, Margaret feels like she's being pulled in two different directions. On the one hand she thrives on the excitement and sense of accomplishment that she gets from growing a successful company; on the other, she longs to be with her boys while they're growing up. The stress of this conflict is starting to wear her down. It's hard enough juggling what feels like two full-time jobs (her business and her family), but the added pressure of this inner turmoil makes it unbearable. Margaret knows that something's got to give.

Although the details of your life may be different, the feelings of frustration, exhaustion, and loneliness may be all too familiar. For many of us who live in a fast-paced, adrenaline-fueled society, questions about meaning, purpose, and true happiness are faithful companions in the day-to-day creation of our lives. We long for something more. Years of searching for happiness and fulfillment in the external world of work have taken their toll. We've lost ourselves in the daily madness of our busy lives.

As a personal coach I became a partner with my clients, and during our weekly meetings I'd help them to reevaluate their priorities, redefine success based on a more holistic perspective of life, and take the necessary actions to bring about the positive changes they desired. Each week clients would leave with an action plan, and I quickly noticed that the small weekly homework assignments started to make a big difference. One client, who had lived in a chaotic, cluttered environment for years, started creating order out of chaos and regained a whole new perspective on his life. Another client, who had suffered from the heavy burden of debt created by years of financial irresponsibility, began to make small weekly changes that improved her financial health, and her savings started to grow.

During my time working with clients I learned a lot about

what prevents us from living authentic, meaningful lives. And as I shifted my attention from working with individuals to working with groups, I received a lot of feedback on what was holding them back as well. In December 1998 I published *Take Time for Your Life* in order to share this knowledge with a larger audience. In this book I took readers through the same coaching process that I used with clients in my private practice. The steps in the book were designed to help readers take a realistic look at their lives and to help them evaluate what needed to change in order for them to feel happier and to live a higher-quality life.

For example, I encouraged readers to begin making self-care a top priority, so they could make proactive life choices instead of reactive ones. I led them through a process of getting their priorities straight, identifying and eliminating those things that were draining their energy, and investing in their financial health, so they would feel more fully in charge of their lives. I introduced readers to the challenges of living in an adrenaline-crazed society, and I showed them how to slow down and begin exchanging unhealthy forms of fuel, like caffeine, sugar, and anxiety, for healthier forms, like a supportive community and a personalized spiritual practice.

I also went out on the road speaking about these topics to larger audiences who felt disillusioned with their lives. As I spoke to audience members and read through the letters and e-mails I received from readers of my first book, it was clear that these strategies were working and that my readers wanted more. They wanted to continue to hear about others who were making changes in their lives, and they wanted bite-sized homework that they could implement on a weekly basis to support them in making the changes I had outlined in the book. That's when I decided to use technology to my advantage.

In January of 1999 I launched an on-line newsletter called *Life Makeover for the Year 2000*. I designed the newsletter to support readers by providing simple, practical strategies that they could use to improve their personal and professional lives on a weekly basis. Based on my experience while coaching clients, I decided to use the "one week at a time" process not only to help make change easier for more people, but to make the process fun and effective as well. Each week I chose a random topic that addressed a certain area of personal or professional growth, and I added a specific action that readers could take during the week to help improve this area. As readers began taking action, their lives started to change. And all of the small changes they were making started to add up.

The Life Makeover community began to grow as readers started forwarding the weekly newsletters to friends, family members, coworkers, and colleagues around the world. For example, one woman, the dean of a well-known university, distributed the newsletter to everyone at her school. Another reader, the president of a manufacturing company, decided to send the weekly newsletter to every employee at the company. What started out as a community of a few hundred quickly grew to several thousand within one year.

The foundation of this weekly process was rooted in my basic coaching philosophy of extreme self-care. This concept, introduced to me by my colleague, Thomas Leonard, challenged readers to take such good care of themselves that at times the program even felt a bit self-indulgent. There was an important reason for this. In my experience as a coach I learned that when clients took extremely good care of themselves by doing things like taking time off on a regular basis, saying no more often to people or projects or situations that drained them, and listening to and acting on their inner wisdom, their stress levels went down and their life satisfaction increased. They also began to care for others in a much healthier way. This realization became my guiding vision—to help people care more deeply for themselves so they were better able to care for others and the world around them.

THE "LIFE MAKEOVER" PROGRAM is a powerful year-long program for change. It is designed to support you in changing *your* life one week at a time. Each chapter (week) consists of a topic of the week and contains a Take Action Challenge and a Resources section to support you in taking action quickly and easily. (Many of these resources were provided by our online community.)

The process is meant to be simple and fun. Although I have kept the original theme of starting at the beginning of the year (January) and working through until the end (December), I invite you to use this book in your own unique way. Whether you decide to start from the beginning and work from Week #1 through Week #52, dip into the book at random, or find a chapter that covers a topic you'd like to work on, what matters most of all is that you *do* something with the material you read. After all, taking action is the only way to create positive, long-lasting change in your life. As you begin to engage in the weekly Take Action Challenge homework, you'll see how one week builds upon another, and before you know it, you'll start to experience important positive changes in your life too!

As you begin this weekly program, the most powerful motivating force that will help you to take the actions outlined in this book is a partner or group of like-minded friends who are interested in changing their lives for the better too. I can't stress this point enough. Community is an extremely important ingredient for your success. Partnering with a coworker, family member, or friend is like providing yourself with a life-insurance policy that will pay far greater dividends. You might even create your own book club, work-study group, or family team. Once you have your partner or team in place, follow these four simple guidelines:

1. Make a plan for how you'll support each other. For example, will you meet in person or over the phone? How often will you meet and when?

2. Review the topic of the week and discuss how the topic relates to you and your life.

3. Make a commitment to a specific action related to the "Take Action Challenge" and let your partner or team know what you'll be working on during the week.

4. Plan a time to reconnect so you can share your progress and celebrate your success together.

Don't be afraid to ask for support during the week. In the beginning you might need a helping hand more often. These simple stories of inspiration and action can make a world of difference in your life and the lives of those you care about. It only takes one small consistent action to make a big change in your life, so don't let fear, procrastination, or doubt get in your way.

As you start to make changes on a weekly basis, be prepared for your life to unfold in wonderful ways. As you clean up the clutter, reconnect with your inner wisdom, strengthen your character, and take on the challenges of high-quality living, you'll find that the lost parts of yourself start to come together to form a pretty amazing life. Good luck!

THE JOURNEY BEGINS!

Love yourself first and everything else falls into line.
LUCILLE BALL

I t's the beginning of the Life Makeover journey, and I imagine you've already begun thinking about the changes you'd like to make in your life. Or maybe you have a sense that something needs to change but you're not sure what it might be. So often when we launch a new beginning in our lives, we start out by setting goals or making resolutions. But I'd like you to start this journey in a different way. I'd like you to begin by acknowledging yourself for what you've already accomplished and, more importantly, who you've become over the last year.

A high-quality life starts with a high-quality you! Don't rush into this new year frantically trying to catch up or make up for what you didn't do in the past. This kind of frenetic rushing and hopeless browbeating keeps you tied to the past and feeling bad about yourself. Get a fresh start on this process by being gentle with yourself. Set aside some time to reflect on all you've done *right* over the last year by considering the following questions:

- What qualities of character have you strengthened? Are you more honest with others about how you feel? Have you learned to set boundaries with those people who drain your energy? Maybe you've improved your communication skills or become more sensitive to the needs of others?

- Have you shared an act of kindness or supported others in some way? Did you help a friend who is going through a divorce or care for an elderly parent? Maybe you coached your kid's sports team or volunteered for a non-profit organization?

- What special memories have you created with those you love? Did you take a vacation that was particularly memorable? Did you organize an event that brought people closer together? Were there any special moments that stand out?

- What have you achieved or accomplished? Consider both your personal and professional life. Did you meet your business goals or get a promotion at work? Maybe you finished an important project, like writing a book or developing a workshop, or channeled your creative energy into painting or cooking?

The answers to these questions will help to start the process off in a different frame of mind—one that is self-supporting and sustainable. After all, we don't grow in positive ways by beating ourselves up. Focus on what worked, and set the stage for a wonderful new year!

TAKE ACTION CHALLENGE

I'd like you to start this process by keeping a journal. Take some time this week to buy yourself a special gift. You'll be using this journal throughout the Life Makeover process to capture your journey, so make sure that you choose one that you really like.

For the first entry reflect on the previous year and make a list of twenty-five (yes, twenty-five!) things you are most proud of accomplishing over the last twelve months. This list may include ways that you've grown as a person, goals you've achieved, and the positive changes that you've made in your life.

Let this exercise be easy. Keep a sheet of paper in your desk, taped to your bathroom mirror, or in your appointment book, and over the next week add items as they occur to you. You might even build a new habit by considering these accomplishments during the same time each day. For example, upon waking, spend a few minutes in bed reviewing the last year in your mind looking for what you did well. Or use the time while you're brushing your teeth or commuting to work to consider your accomplishments. By the end of the week you may even have more than 25 — that's allowed!

When you've completed the list, share it with your partner or team. Better yet, hold a bragging party and invite several people to gather and share their lists. Taking the time to acknowledge your accomplishments and celebrate your success is an important way to strengthen the relationship with yourself, the first step in creating the life you want.

And for those of you who might fear that this exercise is a tad self-indulgent, remember this: seeing the good in others starts with seeing the good in ourselves.

My five most important accomplishments are:

1. _____

2. _____

3. _____

4. _____

5. _____

The three ways I've grown over the last year are:

1. _____

2. _____

3. _____

RESOURCES

Brushdance
100 Ebbtide Ave., #1
Sausalito, CA 94965
(800) 531–7445
http://www.brushdance.com

A great resource for journals as well as electronic greeting cards, magnets, calendars, and new paper greeting cards, too.

What You Need to Know Now — a Road Map for Personal Transformation (tape and CD) by Marcia Pear
To order:
Live Your Light Foundation
(707) 522–9529
http://www.liveyourlight.com

A wonderful spoken-word adventure (with music) that demystifies the evolutionary path and provides practical tools and next steps for dealing with life changes and transitions.

The 12 Secrets of Highly Creative Women: A Portable Mentor by Gail McMeekin (California: Conari Press, 2000)

This book profiles forty-five modern-day creative women (Sarah Ban Breathnach, Barbara Sher, Clarissa Pinkola Estes, and more) and shares their twelve secrets of success.

How Much Joy Can You Stand? How to Push Past Your Fears and Create Your Dreams by Suzanne Falter-Barns (New York: Wellspring, 2000)

This book provides the kick in the pants we all need to get on with our dreams. Not only does it debunk the myths about creating, but it also provides fun, inspiring exercises that work!

Making Your Dreams Come True by Marcia Wieder (New York: Harmony Books, 1999)

An inspiring step-by-step approach for igniting your passion and getting what you want.

NEW YEAR/NEW YOU

*The world rewards those who take responsibility for
their own success.*

CURT GERRISH

Now that you've had a chance to celebrate your accomplishments and growth over the past year, it's time to set a new kind of goal. Instead of thinking about the things that you'd like to bring into your life throughout this process, or the things you'd like to get rid of, do something a bit different. I'd like to suggest that you set an *internal* goal; one that focuses on how you'll develop yourself personally or strengthen your character during the next year.

Long-lasting change starts on the inside. By focusing your attention on things like becoming more honest, bold, or creative, you'll find that the how-to of achieving your goals gets a whole lot easier. As you strengthen yourself from the inside out, it's as if you were brightening your internal light. And as this light shines brighter, you'll probably find that you begin to attract opportunities and resources that support your external goals.

What quality would you like to develop more of over the next year? How do you need to grow? If you're unsure of where to focus, here are some examples:

This year I intend to:

Become financially responsible

Reassess and focus on my top priorities

Be patient

Be more loving and kind

Be better able to set boundaries and say no

Be courageous, fearless, and bold

Be open-minded

Be grateful

Be proactive instead of reactive

Be adventurous

Be trusting and faithful

Once you've chosen the quality you'd like to focus on, follow this three-step process:

Step 1. Write a positive affirmation in the present tense that relates to this goal.

Step 2. Print this affirmation on a piece of paper and hang it in your home or office.

Step 3. Choose three actions you can take during the next week to begin developing this quality right away.

Now let's look at a couple of examples.

Let's imagine that you've decided to become a more financially responsible person this year. You might create an affirmation that says:

"I enjoy being a financially responsible person"

Next, post this affirmation some place where you'll see it often. Then create your action steps for the week. You might decide to balance your accounts, create a debt-elimination plan, and make an appointment with a financial adviser.

Now let's imagine that the quality you've chosen is to become more focused. You might create an affirmation that says:

"I focus my attention on my top three priorities every day."

And once you've hung up this affirmation, you set your actions in place. You might shut the ringer off on your phone for two hours a day so that you can focus on the work that needs to get done. You could set clear boundaries with employees to prevent interruptions. And you could create a morning ritual whereby you identify and eliminate any possible distractions that might prevent you from focusing on what's important for the day.

As you consider the quality you'd like to develop, remember that the quickest way to create a better life is to focus on becoming a better you. Make the development of this quality your top priority and intentionally focus on the steps that will bring this change about. Once you choose a quality, you'll probably find that the universe presents you with plenty of opportunities to practice. Don't worry! Stand tall and face these challenges head on. The sooner you do, the quicker you'll step into a whole new way of being in the world.

If you start each week with a plan for how you'll continue to develop the quality you've chosen, you'll reap great rewards. You'll find that your confidence increases, you trust (and follow) your gut instinct more often, and your goals seem to get accomplished with far less effort. By focusing on the *who*, you'll probably find that the *what* takes care of itself. And the truth is that it's much easier to take a proactive approach to growth by *choosing* how you'll develop yourself than it is to wait for life to throw you a few curve balls in the form of lessons. Happy New You!

TAKE ACTION CHALLENGE

Using your journal, take some time this week to write about who you are at this time in your life in relation to the quality that you'd like to develop. For example, if you feel as though you're someone who is afraid of new experiences, write about your fears and concerns now. This exercise will provide a frame of reference to mark your progress as you review your journal throughout the year.

Once you've chosen the quality you'd most like (or need) to develop this year, follow the three-step process above. Keep your affirmation in clear view and start each week by identifying three action steps that will help you to grow. Then, make sure you take action!

The quality I'd most like to develop is:

_____

My affirmation is:

_____

The three actions I will take this week are:

1. _____

2. _____

3. _____

RESOURCES

The Life We Are Given by George
Leonard and Michael Murphy
(New York: Putnam, 1995)

A long-term program for realizing
the potential of body, mind, heart,
and soul.

Love Precious Humanity by Kayt
Kennedy, Editor (Florida: Star's
Edge International, 1999)

The collected wisdom of Harry
Palmer, creator of Avatar—self-
evolvement, self-development,
self-empowerment courses that are
delivered in fifty-eight countries.

Lifewise Living Daily Calendar by
Rebecca Lang and Jeri Engen
Creative Health Designs
4615 80th Place
Urbandale, IA 50322
(515) 276–4764

A wonderful collection of motiva-
tional thoughts and actions.

FINDING YOUR LOST SELF

When you're in solitary confinement and you're six feet under without light, sound, or running water, there is no place to go but inside. And when you go inside, you discover that everything that exists in the Universe is also within you.

RUBIN CARTER, *THE HURRICANE*

In my years of working as a coach, I often hear people say that they feel as though something is missing from their lives. And usually it's very difficult for them to pinpoint exactly what it is. Whether it's a friend talking about feeling unfulfilled at work or a reader who asks for help in finding her lost self amid the daily madness of work and raising a family, it seems that many of us are struggling to find more meaning and a sense of purpose in our lives.

If you feel dissatisfied with your life, or if you feel as though something is missing, you might want to consider this . . . it might just be that what's missing from your life is *you.*

We live in a world that continuously pulls us outside of ourselves. Between the media, our jobs, and life's responsibilities, our vision always seems to be turned outward. As I see it, this is the main reason why so many people feel off course or as though they're not traveling down the "right" path. You see, the most accurate compass—our inner wisdom—resides within. So, when we spend so much of our lives focused on what's "out there," we end up feeling lost and confused.

Think of it this way. Imagine that your life is a giant wheel, with spokes that reach out and touch every area of your life—work, relationships, family, community, health, and the like. At the center of this wheel is a core of knowledge, wisdom, and experience called *you*. The more connected you are to this center, the more you'll be linked to your values, needs, and desires. And the more your life begins to take on a deeper sense of meaning and purpose.

In order to capture the "something" that seems to be missing, you'll need to get to know your inner self in the same way you'd get to know a new lover or friend—you invest a sufficient amount of time and attention in this important relationship. There are many paths that will lead you to your Self. Here are just a few examples:

1. *Keep a journal.* Trust me, I'll sound like a broken record when it comes to recommending this step, but it's such a powerful way to reestablish a relationship with yourself that it's worth repeating. Write your life story. Write about what's working or what isn't working in your life. Just write *something* in order to start an ongoing dialogue with yourself.

2. *Capture your dreams.* Just for a moment forget about your conscious dreams and goals. Keep track of the dreams that take place while you're asleep. Dreams are a doorway to our inner life. They often reflect our deepest longings, hopes, and fears. If you were to begin writing down your dreams (even the fragments you barely remember), you'd learn a lot about yourself pretty quickly. And, if you're reading this and saying, "But I don't dream" or "I don't remember my dreams," don't worry. Once you start capturing even the slightest dream thoughts or fragments, your

subconscious mind gets the message that you're paying attention and rewards you with a better dream memory.

3. *Create a community of support.* Invite a small group of trusted friends to join you in this search for self. Set up a regular meeting and use this time to share what you're learning about yourself with others. Having a safe place to share your thoughts and feelings will help you to uncover valuable information about who you are and what you've come here to do.

4. *Reawaken your spiritual life.* Dedicate some time each day to your spiritual life. Study spiritually inspiring literature like the Bible, the Torah, or the Bhagavad Gita. Study the teachings of Jesus Christ, Sai Baba, or the Dalai Lama. Return to the rituals and prayers that may have once provided comfort and divine connection. Write letters to God in your journal. This daily practice will keep you surrounded in an atmosphere of spirit and will help you to hear the voice of your soul more clearly.

Although these examples are great ways to find your lost self, what matters more than anything is this:

> *When you make a promise to spend time with yourself you must keep your promise!*

Show up. Schedule time with yourself on a regular basis, and increase the duration and frequency over time. If you're not used to being alone with yourself, there's a good chance that this time alone will feel a bit uncomfortable, even boring at first. But hang in there. In our culture, turning your vision inward can feel like defying gravity. You're attempting to do the opposite of what the world is trying to get you to do. If you hang on through the discomfort, you will reach a point when you look forward to spending time alone.

Your relationship to yourself is at the heart of a great career, loving relationships, true joy, and a meaningful life. It all begins with you. If you feel like something's missing from *your* life, move to the center and reclaim your wise and wonderful Self.

TAKE ACTION CHALLENGE

Take out your date book or calendar and get ready to schedule appointments for you! For the next six months block out some time each week and mark it off in ink. As you schedule this time, increase the amount from month to month. For example, if you start out with an hour a week for the first month, expand that time to an evening or afternoon for the second month.

Remember that as soon as you schedule this time, chances are pretty good that someone will challenge your commitment. Stay strong! Although there will obviously be times when you'll need to rearrange your schedule, set a new standard that honors your Self first by limiting the interruptions.

RESOURCES

A Woman's Journey to God by Joan Borysenko (New York: Riverhead Books, 2000)

This is a beautifully written book, which will help you to reawaken your spiritual life.

The Creative Dreamer's Journal and Workbook by Veronica Tonay (Berkeley, California: Celestial Arts, 1997)

This book is half journal and half workbook, with exercises to help illuminate the meaning of your dreams.

I Could Do Anything If I Only Knew What It Was: How to Discover What You Really Want and How to Get It by Barbara Sher with Barbara Smith (New York: Delacorte Press, 1994).

This book reveals how to recapture long-lost goals, overcome the blocks that inhibit your success, decide what you want to be, and live your dreams.

The Whole Person Fertility Program by Niravi B. Payne, M.S., and Brenda Lane Richardson (New York: Three Rivers Press, 1998)

Although this book is geared toward fertility issues, it provides highly effective exercises to get to know yourself better and identify and work through emotional-based roadblocks to self-growth, creativity, health, and fertility.

Writing Your Authentic Self by Lois Guarino (New York: Dell Books, 1999)

This book presents step-by-step advice on keeping every type of journal, from a personal diary to a dream chronicle.

Week 4

THE CHALLENGE

*Morning pages do get us to the other side: the other side of
our fear, of our negativity, of our moods. Above all, they get
us beyond our Censor. Beyond the reach of the Censor's
babble we find our own quiet center, the place where we
hear the still, small voice that is at once our creator's
and our own.*

JULIA CAMERON

I've been writing in a journal since the age of thirteen and have always found it to be an enormous source of comfort and connection to my Self. For years my journal writing has been somewhat sporadic—sometimes days would go by, weeks, and even months between entries. Other times I'd write page after page, day after day.

Recently, as a result of a promise to my best friend Max, I decided to renew my commitment to write every morning as an experiment to see how the practice might affect my life. The results have been amazing, and I wanted to share some of them with you in the hopes that you too might be inspired to participate in the "Take Action Challenge" at the end of this chapter. But first, the results. . . .

Since I've been writing every day I've found that

1. I feel deeply connected to my soul and what really matters.

2. My days are consistently oriented around my top priorities.

3. Synchronistic events occur to support these priorities.

4. I feel a sense of security that no outside force has ever given me.

5. My eating habits have improved dramatically.

6. My choices are more inner-directed, I care less about what others think.

7. I care more about spending time alone.

In the past, when I'd heard Julia Cameron, author of *The Artist's Way*, talk about the power of using "morning pages" (writing a minimum of three pages every morning by hand), I agreed that this was a smart exercise, but I never committed to the three pages *every* morning by hand. Now that I have, it's become an important part of my daily spiritual practice and I find that I actually *need* to write.

Often when I suggest to audiences or clients that they keep a journal, they have lots of questions. Usually these questions cover three areas.

1. *When is the best time to write?* I always recommend writing in the morning because chances are that it's the closest you'll get to hearing the voice of your soul—your inner wisdom—before your busy day kicks in. When you journal at the end of the day, your mind is full, and you're more likely to spend time reporting on events rather than writing about how you feel. If the mornings are difficult for some reason, make an effort to at least do *some* writing before the start of your day, even if it's just one page.

2. *What should I write?* If you find that you have a difficult time getting started because you're not sure about what to write, don't

worry. Most of the questions I receive about journal writing deal with this very issue. The trick is to get started. Think of your daily writing practice as developing a new relationship. Sometimes, when you first meet someone, you don't quite know what to say. But after a while the words start to flow. To help you get started, try using the following sentence stems:

This morning I feel . . .

I'm always daydreaming about . . .

My nagging inner voice keeps telling me to . . .

The thoughts that roll around in my head are . . .

My soul longs to . . .

What I'm most afraid of is . . .

My inner critic tells me . . .

What I'm most grateful for is . . .

Keep your pen on the page and write down the thoughts that enter your mind. It takes practice and patience. It will get easier over time. When you feel stuck and unable to write, write about feeling stuck.

3. *How can I stay motivated to write?* One of the most important things I did to help me shift from "Daily writing is a nuisance" to "I can't wait to write," was to create a comfortable writing place. Choose a room (or section of a room) and do what's necessary to make it the kind of place you'll look forward to spending time in. For example, find a comfortable chair and good lighting. Add a few candles, some incense, a lap desk, or maybe a favorite blanket. I've found that by creating a sacred place to write my body automatically moves toward the comfort and solitude that this space has to offer.

If something happens and you miss a day, don't let that stop you. Just get up the next morning and start again. You're learning to connect your head with your heart by writing about how you *feel*. Not only will this daily ritual help you to develop more control over your actions; it will also ignite the kind of synchronicity that leads to a better life. You see, when you are more regularly connected to your inner self, you tend to act on its wisdom more often. This produces synchronistic events. But don't take my word for it. Read on, take the challenge, and see what shows up in *your* life.

TAKE ACTION CHALLENGE

Choose a thirty-day period and commit to writing a minimum of three pages every morning by hand. Hold this time as sacred and see it as an opportunity to connect with your inner wisdom — your Wise Self. Don't worry about what to say, punctuation, spelling, being brilliant, or whether or not you can fill the page. Find a safe place to keep your journal where no one will find it, and simply write. When you feel as though you have nothing to say, just keep your hand moving anyway — you might be surprised at what shows up.

RESOURCES

The Artist's Way by Julia Cameron and Mark Bryan (New York: J. P. Tarcher, 1992)

If you long to unleash and use your creative self, then this resource is a must.

Reflections on the Artist's Way, an interview with Julia Cameron, audio cassette (Sounds True, November 1993)

A wonderful interview with Julia Cameron in which she talks about identifying what you love and dedicating yourself to cultivating your creativity.

All About Me by Philipp Keel (New York: Broadway Books, 1998)

A unique "fill in the blanks" book that will help you to know yourself better and share yourself with others.

Michael Roger Press, Inc.
Middlesex, NJ 08846
(732) 752–0800
www.bookbinders.com

A wide variety of innovative lined and unlined blank books. This company can also craft custom designs and cover materials.

Running Rhino
P. O. Box 24843
Seattle, WA 98124
(206) 284–2868
www.runningrhino.com

This company has a beautiful selection of journals that you can view on-line.

THE GIFT OF TIME

Time is a created thing. To say "I don't have time"
is like saying, "I don't want to . . ."

LAO-TZU

'm always surprised by the number of people who ask, "Where does all the time go, and why don't we have enough?" If you're like me, you've probably asked yourself the same question. Sometimes it seems as though a "time bandit" steals our minutes when we're not looking, only to leave us feeling frustrated and regretful at the end of the week.

The truth is that we control where our time goes. Time is finite. We only get a certain amount—168 hours a week, fifty-two weeks a year, and that's if we don't die first. Time is a gift that most of us take for granted. We get so caught up in the busyness of our daily lives that we rarely stop and take a serious look at how we're spending this gift.

When is the last time you stopped to consider where your time is being spent and how you feel about it? How long do you *really* work in a week? How much time do you spend caring for others? How much of your time is spent caring for yourself?

Most of us work an average of fifty-five hours a week (I'm being generous here) if we count the time spent at the office, commuting, preparing for work, and worrying about work. And that's not counting the twenty-four-hours-a-day job of parenting for those of you with children! If we add to that an average of fifty hours per week spent sleeping, we're left with sixty-three hours for shopping, cooking, cleaning, exercising, self-care, errands, fun, friends, family, volunteering, and so on. It's no wonder that time seems in short supply.

When you realize that *you* are in charge of your life and your time is limited, your choices become more important. You'll care more about what you say yes to and what you say no to.

One of the ways to take control of where you spend your time is to create what I call an Absolute Yes list. This is a list of the top five priorities that need your attention for the next three to six months. Unlike goals or dreams, the first place to focus your time and energy when building a strong foundation for your life is on those things that need your attention *now*. For example, there may be a relationship that you've been neglecting because of overworking that needs your attention in order to heal. Or you may feel financially strapped or overburdened with debt and need to focus on improving the state of your financial health so that you can make the kind of choices that will improve your life.

Creating an Absolute Yes list will help you to remember your priorities, especially when your life gets hectic and you feel like you're losing time. Having this list handy makes it easier to focus your time on the things that are most important, and in doing so, to identify the things that are a waste of your time. After all, once you're clear about the yeses, the nos become easier to define too! Then, when you find yourself wondering where all the time goes, remember this: if you don't say yes, the schedule doesn't fill.

TAKE ACTION CHALLENGE

This week you get to create your own Absolute Yes list. Start by choosing a quiet afternoon or evening when you'll have at least an hour of uninterrupted time to yourself. Have your journal handy, and during this time get comfortable and relax.

While in a relaxed state, ask yourself the following two questions, giving yourself ample time for each one:

What needs my attention at this time in my life?

What do I need to let go of?

Don't censor your answers. Instead, just notice what occurs to you as you ponder each of these questions separately and write the answers down in your journal. If, when doing this exercise, you don't get any answers, don't worry. Just stop and consider the different areas of your life—relationships, family, community, work, emotional and physical health, finances, and so on—and make a note of those things that you know need your attention.

When you're finished, choose the top five answers and put them in order of priority. Next, copy this list onto several 3x5-inch index cards and label it "My Absolute Yes List." Place these index cards in various places around your home and office. For example, you might place one by the phone, one on your bathroom mirror, one near your computer, and one even on the dashboard of your car. Keeping this list nearby will remind you of what really matters and will challenge you to say no to those things that are not on the list.

The process of creating an Absolute Yes list (which can also be used separately for your work-related priorities) should be repeated every three to six months, so that you have an updated list of your top priorities. Once you know your priorities, challenge yourself to say no to at least two requests of your time each day this week. For example, when a colleague asks for your help with a project, graciously decline, citing the need to get your own work completed. Or when a friend calls to complain about a problem, tell him or her that they have two minutes to complain, and then you'd like to know what they're going to do about it.

Learning to say no with grace and love is a key way to protect your gift of time. If saying no is difficult for you (as it is for most people), remember the following three tips:

1. Your self-care is always a valid excuse.

2. You don't need to overexplain or defend your actions. Just tell the simple truth.

3. Doing things out of guilt and obligation is not doing things out of love.

So, the next time someone asks you to do something that you'd rather not do, simply smile and tell them you're not available.

RESOURCES

Time Shifting, Creating More Time for Your Life by Stephan Rechtschaffen (New York: Doubleday, 1997)

Rechtschaffen teaches the reader how to "time shift"—move in rhythm with others, stretch the present, and practice mindfulness.

Moms Network
http://www.momsnetwork.com

This site provides enormous resources that help work-at-home and stay-at-home moms find balance in their lives through discussion lists, message boards, information, and more.

At-Home Dad Network
http://www.Athomedad.com

This site provides a newsletter, network, and resources devoted to fathers who stay home with their children.

Your Heart's Desire: Instructions for Creating the Life You Really Want by Sonia Choquette, Patrick Tully, and Julia Cameron (New York: Crown, 1997)

This book provides a practical guide that helps you to identify what's important enough to give your time to.

How to Say the Tough Stuff
(audio program) by G. Lyn Allen
G. Lyn Allen
P. O. Box 8792
Shreveport, LA 71148
(318) 686-4551
http://www.lynallen.com

Two hours of practical techniques and information intended to support you in feeling better about saying the tough stuff immediately.

Tuesdays with Morrie, by Mitch Albom (New York: Doubleday, 1977)

An inspiring and motivating reminder of what really matters.

How to Say No Without Feeling Guilty: And Say Yes to More Time, More Joy, and What Matters Most to You by Patti Breitman and Connie Hatch (New York: Doubleday, Broadway, 2000)

The ultimate "No" guide.

WHAT'S DRAINING YOU?

*Within each of us is a hidden store of energy. Energy we
can release to compete in the marathon of life.*

ROGER DAWSON

In *Take Time for Your Life* I dedicated a chapter to identifying and eliminating energy drains as a way to replenish our energy and renew our enthusiasm for life. The concept of eliminating what drains you is a powerful one. In the past, when working with clients, I often recommended that we focus the first three to six months of our work together on this one idea alone. By getting rid of the things that were draining a client's energy, the client was emotionally and physically freed up, and as a result they began to attract better things into their lives.

For example, when I first began working with Lisa, a CPA from a small accounting firm, she was surprised to hear that my recommended strategy for increasing her client base (her primary goal) was to clean up the piles of files that decorated her office floor. I knew from past experience during my tax-consulting days that the client files left around the office drained her energy whether she was in her office or not. These files represented unfinished work that needed to get handled, and anytime she even thought about them, she immediately felt weighed down.

Even though Lisa wanted to add new clients to her firm, this added weight actually kept them away. Lisa even admitted that each time her phone rang, she felt herself cringe at the additional work that might be on the other end of the line. Until Lisa felt freed up emotionally by eliminating the unfinished work, there was a good chance that she would block herself from adding new clients.

Once Lisa dedicated time to handling these files and eliminating the piles of paperwork, new clients started to show up almost like clockwork. One day in particular, after finishing her to-do list and putting all of her files in a filing cabinet, she actually had three calls from new clients in one afternoon! And because her office had been cleared of the piles, she felt more confident in her ability to handle more work, and this confidence made her much more attractive to potential clients.

It's amazing what eliminating energy drains can do to our mood. Remember how good you felt when you finally went through your closet and cleaned out the old clothes that you were sure you'd wear again someday? Or, finally paid the bills that you had been avoiding in your "bills to be paid" file? Once we go through and plug these energy drains, especially the ones that cause us anxiety and stress, we free up enormous amounts of energy to be used for better things.

Although eliminating energy drains can be about the importance of removing unwanted clutter, getting organized, or handling the little annoyances of day-to-day living (topics we'll cover in future chapters), this week I'd like you to focus on identifying and eliminating the energy drains that have emotional strings attached—the kind of drains that cause you to feel emotionally distressed, anxious or overburdened. These energy drains cost too much.

To identify the energy drains that might have emotional strings attached, ask yourself the following questions:

- Is there a phone call I need to make or a conversation I need to have that I keep avoiding?

- Have I said yes to a commitment that I now regret?

- Am I involved in a project that no longer holds my interest?

- Is there something I'm doing that I know should be delegated to someone else?

- Am I pursuing a goal that no longer makes sense?

- Am I holding on to something in my home or office that represents a difficult time in my life or that keeps me attached to the past?

- Am I dealing with a sick child or an aging parent alone?

The answers to these questions may reveal important energy drains that need to be handled. For example, when you keep pursuing a business that's not succeeding regardless of what you do, the effort steals your energy. When you hang on to files that contain divorce papers, old financial records, cards from former lovers, or college textbooks that represent a career you didn't pursue, these items can keep you tied to the past and may actually prevent you from moving on with your life. And when you're dealing with the most emotionally challenging energy drains of all, such as a sick child or an aging parent, trying to do it all alone will steal the energy you need to be there for your loved one.

When you finally let go of the past or handle the items that cause you anxiety, that action alone can have a dramatic positive impact on your life. For example, freeing up your energy and eliminating your anxiety makes you more productive and effective at work. Or your relationships grow stronger because you're able to be present for others. And not only do you *feel* better, but you also make physical and mental space for great things to come into your life, like a new friend or romantic partner, a new job, or even more money.

Now that you realize the cost of these types of energy drains and the benefits of getting them handled, it's time to take action!

TAKE ACTION CHALLENGE

This week we'll focus on eliminating some of the energy drains that have been draining you physically and emotionally. Using the four-step process below, free yourself from the emotional strings that bind you!

1. Scan your environment for five energy drains that have emotional strings attached. Consider the things in your home or office, relationship issues that might be draining you, or work-related problems that need to be handled.

2. Schedule time to handle these five items.

3. As you prepare to handle them, make sure you get support for those things that you'd rather avoid. For example, if going through old records or items from the past causes you to feel upset or nervous, ask a friend to sit with you as you weed through them.

4. Break the tasks into small steps and get to work.

5. Build in a reward. Once you've finished a task, do something enjoyable to reward yourself and to motivate you to continue with the process.

The five energy drains with emotional strings attached are:

1. _____

2. _____

3. _____

4. _____

5. _____

I plan to handle these items on _____ at _____.

The person I can call to support me with this project is:

_____

When I'm finished, I'll reward myself by doing:

_____

RESOURCES

Energy Anatomy by Caroline Myss
(six-cassette audio program)
Sounds True
413 S. Arthur Avenue
Louisville, CO 80027
(800) 333–9185

A great resource for understanding a different view of how our life energy is used.

Creating Sacred Space with Feng Shui: Learn the Art of Space Clearing and Bring New Energy into Your Life by Karen Kingston (New York: Broadway Books, 1997)

Provides simple and effective techniques on how to create harmony and abundance by clearing and enhancing home and workplace energies and explains the link between inner peace and the buildings in which we live.

David Allen & Co.
P.O. Box 27705
Raleigh, NC 27611
(805) 646–8432
www.davidallenonline.com

David's site has great information on getting organized and working more effectively.

Sacred Space: Clearing and Enhancing the Energy of Your Home by Denise Linn (New York: Ballantine Books, January 1996)

An all-time favorite book on creating sacred space.

THE MAGIC OF GRACE

Seekers are offered clues all the time from the world of the spirit. Ordinary people call these clues coincidences.

DEEPAK CHOPRA

This week's topic is about motivation—the kind of fuel that will inspire you to take action consistently to create the life you want. The way I see it, there are three things that will help you to stay on the Life Makeover path: a partner, successful results, and the magic of grace.

As you embark on your journey, using the support of a partner who is excited about making positive changes in his or her life will help both of you to stay in action. Remember, action creates change. It's time to stop thinking about the changes you want to make and start doing something about them! Certainly the best type of partner would be a well-trained, experienced coach but if you cannot afford a coach yet, make this process a game and ask a friend, colleague, or family member to play. Even better, gather a group of friends, coworkers, or family members and go through the process together. Then, as you take action and begin experiencing positive results in your life, the excitement, relief, or added energy you feel will also motivate you to continue moving forward on the Life Makeover path. These two ingredients provide important sources of motivation.

The best motivating factor of all, however, is divine intervention, or what I like to call The Magic of Grace. As you take action and make changes in your life, you'll probably find that co-incidences start occurring all around you. For example, you might suddenly receive a piece of information in the mail that will allow you to move forward with an important decision. Or you might have a conversation with a friend and hear the exact piece of advice needed to help solve a problem. These synchronistic events are a direct result of investing in your life and practicing these self-care strategies.

Experience has taught me that when we treat ourselves like cherished souls, a divine force supports our efforts. Because I've witnessed this phenomenon so many times while working with clients (and in my own life), I've come to expect it as a natural part of the journey. When you take steps to honor your Self, like starting a journal, asking for a well-deserved raise, or saying no to unwanted demands on your time, you'll set in motion a higher order for your life. And the best part of all is that you don't have to believe in the magic of grace to reap the rewards. Just take good care of yourself and wait for the miracles; they'll become a very special source of motivation throughout this journey.

TAKE ACTION CHALLENGE

During this next week pay close attention to the coincidences that occur in your life as you make your self-care a higher priority. Notice when something happens that makes your life easier, when something you need magically appears, or when you receive an act of kindness from a stranger. Write about these miracles, large or small, in your journal. By writing them down, you'll come to believe in the magic of grace and begin to expect them in your life too!

RESOURCES

TO FIND A COACH:

Coach University
P.O. Box 881595
Steamboat Springs, CO 80488
(800) 48–COACH
http://www.coachu.com

This coach-training organization offers a coach referral service.

International Coach Federation
1444 I Street NW, Suite 700
Washington, DC 20005
(888) 423–3131
http://www.coachfederation.org

The largest nonprofit professional organization of personal and business coaches that provides an online referral service.

Inspire
www.infoadvn.com/inspire/

For a daily dose of inspiration, you might want to subscribe to the "Inspire" daily broadcast.

Sark's *Magic Museletter*
www.campsark.com/museletter
(415) 546–3742 (voice mail
SARK's "Inspiration Line")

Published quarterly. Subscriptions cost $23, $19.50 for starving artists and children 12 and under. Experience fun and adventure through SARK's colorful artwork, dreams, and imaginings.

WHAT'S FUELING YOU?

It is difficult to live in the present, ridiculous to live in the future, and impossible to live in the past. Nothing is as far away as one minute ago.

JIM BISHOP

Information overload has become the phrase that most people use when they describe the state of being overwhelmed that they feel living in our modern day techno-crazed world. Although "information overload" sounds as if it implied that most people feel buried underneath an enormous amount of paper, conversations with clients and audience members tell me that it means something much more. It means feeling swallowed up by a culture that values quick answers, saving time, and the ability to change and innovate in a nanosecond. Feeling pressured to catch up, keep up, and stay ahead of the curve. Too often we feel as though we're constantly running at full tilt.

The increased speed by which we live has contributed to a society that is suffering from adrenaline overload more than from information overload. When we use adrenaline as our main source of fuel, our body's adrenal system, the fight-or-flight response that is supposed to alert us to and prepare us for danger, never has a chance to rest. It's interesting to note the symbolism of this response to the world we live in. As technology increases and the pace of society quickens, it is as if our "vulnerable inner self" responds to what feels like a dangerous world by staying in a constant state of readiness. This hypervigilant state of fight or flight eventually makes it physiologically difficult to slow down. Technology, which was supposed to make our lives easier, has, in fact, run us into the ground.

Technology is both a blessing and a curse. On one hand it's great that we can pop something to eat in the microwave oven and have a meal prepared in just a few minutes, or that we can communicate with someone on the other side of the world in a flash. Where technology gets us into trouble is when we realize that there are more ways than ever before for people to make requests of our time and attention. For example, every time someone leaves you a voice-mail message, that person has added another to-do item to your already full list. Or, being expected to carry a cell phone or pager for work makes you literally accessible to anyone almost anywhere. And with the addition of e-mail, things have only gotten much worse. In a recent *Fast Company* story, it was reported that the average United States office worker receives over fifty phone calls a day, thirty-five e-mails, and over twenty voice-mail messages, not to mention interoffice memos, faxes, and letters via regular mail. It's no wonder we're burned out!

In addition to being at everyone's beck and call, it sometimes feels as though our bodies actually begin to synchronize to the speed of computers. Remember the last time you upgraded your computer or increased the speed by which you accessed the Internet? How quickly did you become accustomed to the new speed, only to want something even faster? It's no wonder we can't slow down.

There are signals and behaviors that alert us to whether or not we're running on adrenaline. For example, when you end up checking voice mail or e-mail several times a day and feeling a twinge of anxiety while you do it, that's adrenaline kicking in. When you finally have time to yourself and feel so antsy that you end up cleaning a closet or finishing up some work, there's a good chance that adrenaline is making it difficult to slow down and relax. Or when you wake in the middle of the night with thoughts racing through your head, unable to sleep, or feel so distracted during the day that you can't focus well enough to complete your work, it may very well be a signal that adrenaline has become your main source of fuel.

So, how do you restore your energy and begin getting your fuel from a healthier source? Here are some of the things you can do to reduce your reliance on adrenaline and protect your health and well-being.

1. *Get tested.* If you physically feel as though you cannot slow down, then you might want to have your adrenal system tested to see whether or not you need some medical attention to help your body heal. This is important. I've seen too many people fail at using relaxation or meditation techniques because their bodies needed additional supplementation. Contact your doctor and ask to take an adrenal stress index test—a simple saliva test taken throughout one full day.

2. *Schedule some down time.* Whether you schedule fifteen-minute relaxation breaks during the day or put in longer periods of downtime, it's important to begin making space to practice being still.

3. *Change your work habits.* Instead of checking your voice mail or e-mail several times a day, challenge yourself to cut back to once or twice a day. Clear your desk and work on one thing at a time. Turn the ringer off on the phone. Inform others that you've extended your return-message policy. Instead of returning messages within one day, make it one week. At first these behaviors may feel uncomfortable or disorienting, but hang in there. Within

a short amount of time you'll be amazed at how much more re-laxed and focused you feel. If you're worried that these behaviors will only pile up more work, then remember: when there's so much to do that you want to run and hide, it's time to get help. Whether you hire an assistant, request support from your boss, or decide to let go of certain aspects of your work alto-gether, when there's too much to do, there's too much to do.

4. *Breathe deeply.* When we're running on adrenaline, we have a tendency toward shallow breathing. We take quick, short breaths high in the chest and rob our bodies of much-needed oxygen. This lack of oxygen can contribute to things like cold hands, high blood pressure, and anxiety. Start taking mini-self-care breaks throughout the day by breathing deeply using your diaphragm. Place your hand on your lower abdomen and as you breathe, feel this area move in and out. To help you remember to breathe deep, link this practice to daily events. For example, practice deep breathing while driving or at specific periods throughout the day. You might take a few deep breaths to settle yourself at your desk when you arrive in the morning, before you leave for lunch, and again before you leave for home. Increase the frequency, and over time you'll improve the health of your whole nervous system.

5. *Take a good multivitamin* to support your body's immune system.

6. *Give up caffeine.* Many of my clients have been amazed at the amount of energy they have *after* kicking the caffeine habit. Al-though your morning coffee or lunchtime soda may give you a jolt of energy, it wears down your adrenal system over time and actu-ally robs you of energy. Cut back on sugar and junk food, too!

7. *Get regular exercise.* A brisk walk is one of the most favorable things you can do to reduce stress and restore health to your

adrenal system. Start walking to work, taking the stairs, or using your lunch break to get your body moving. Many clients have found that when they link exercise to reducing stress instead of weight loss, they stick with it and automatically get up and move to work off excess energy when they feel anxious or over-stimulated.

The fast-paced nature of our society is only going to speed up even more. As a result you will be challenged to take care of yourself on a whole new level. Take advantage of the information age instead of defending yourself against it, by practicing new behaviors that reduce your reliance on adrenaline so you protect your body, mind and spirit.

TAKE ACTION CHALLENGE

Become aware of the habits and behaviors that keep you hooked on adrenaline. Are you drinking a lot of coffee during the day? Do you spend too much time on the computer? Do you rush from one appointment or task to another?

This week, pick one new behavior from the list above and practice it faithfully during the week. Build on success. Remember: each little change, made over time, will make a big difference in your ability to slow down and improve the quality of your life.

The three habits that keep my adrenaline pumping are:

1. _____

2. _____

3. _____

The one new habit I'll practice this week is:

_____

RESOURCES

Glenn S. Rothfeld, M.D., M.Ac.
Medical Director
Whole Health New England, Inc.
180 Massachusetts Avenue,
Suite 303
Arlington, MA 02474
Phone: (781) 641–1901

Dr. Rothfeld offers an "adrenal stress index" test and provides health consultations by phone.

Adrenaline and Stress: The Exciting New Breakthrough That Helps You Overcome Stress Damage by Dr. Archibald D. Hart (Waco, Texas: World Books, 1995)

Too much stress can produce too much adrenaline, which can be physically damaging. Dr. Hart has discovered the hidden link between adrenaline and stress and shows how to manage adrenaline levels and prevent stress-related illnesses physically, mentally, and spiritually.

8 Weeks to Optimum Health by Andrew Weil (New York: Fawcett Books, 1998)

In this book Dr. Weil offers great breathing techniques and resources for restoring health.

THE POWER OF FOCUS

*When you stay focused and keep a commitment you create
momentum, and momentum creates momentum.*

RICH FETTKE

Sometimes the actions we take in life not only bring success but also teach us new, important ways of being in the world. For example, having a child teaches us to be more patient. Or embarking on a new career path helps us become more courageous.

Completing my first book taught me to focus my energy on one goal at a time. In order to meet each deadline and allow my creative juices to flow, I learned to focus my time and attention on what mattered. In spite of the fear or frustration it caused, I had to constantly say no to things I really wanted to do, miss opportunities that seemed really big, and consistently pull myself back on purpose.

I learned an important lesson: the power of disciplined focus is the secret of success. To focus means to bring your attention to the center, to concentrate on one thing intently in order to gain clarity. Teaching yourself to stay focused on one project, goal, or opportunity at a time will not only allow you to be more productive and effective, it can also challenge you to go more deeply into the task at hand and bring forth more creative insight and wisdom.

Too often we try to "cover all the bases," respond to every opportunity, or provide every possible service that someone might need, in the hopes of striking success. But the truth is, long-term,

47

sustainable success often comes from the ability to stay focused on one project or goal at a time.

To determine whether or not you may be having trouble focusing, answer the following questions:

1. Do you find yourself generating so many new ideas that you never get started on one?

2. Are you easily distracted during the day and feel as though you never get anything completed?

3. Does your business card or brochure list so many products or services that it sometimes confuses potential customers?

We are creative beings. It makes sense that we'd want to pursue many interests or travel several paths at once. But remember that when you expend your energy in several directions, you weaken the power behind one. Is there a project or goal that needs your devoted attention?

TAKE ACTION CHALLENGE

During the next week pick a project or goal and devote your focused energy to it every day. Choose a preplanned amount of time, schedule it in your appointment book, and challenge yourself to stay on purpose. You might decide to use this focused time for something related to self-care, writing an article, or marketing your business. Simply shut the door, turn the ringer off on the phone, post a DO NOT DISTURB sign, or do whatever it takes to keep your attention and action focused on what's important.

Each time you're tempted to sway toward something else (and you will be), bring your attention back to the present. When your mind starts to wander, remind yourself to stay focused by using a simple mantra like: "I do complete work." Using this mantra will help you build your "focus muscle." Once you get better at staying focused, you'll not only be less tempted by distractions, you'll also engage more joyfully in the process of creation.

This week I'll focus my attention on:

_____

RESOURCES

The Power of Focus: **A Guide to Clarity and Achievement** by Rich Fettke (audio tape program)
To order:
http://www.FETTKE.com
1630 North Main Street,
Suite 352
Walnut Creek, CA 94596
(800) 200–COACH (2622)

An inspiring, two-cassette audio-tape program that will help you develop the focus needed to create a more successful, high-quality life.

Focus Your Energy by Thom Hartmann (New York: Pocket Books, 1994)

This book is out of print, but it's so useful that I'd recommend you check your local library or used bookstore (online too). Although this book is designed to guide the ADD-type personality in business situations, it's an excellent resource for all who want to learn to focus their energy in a more productive way.

The Power of Focus by Jack Canfield, Les Hewitt, Mark Victor Hansen (Health Communications, 2000)

This book shares the ten "focusing strategies" the authors used to get their first books published and to build on their success. They include new stories and their own personal anecdotes to show the importance of having successful habits, creating balance, and maintaining confidence.

The Focusing Institute
34 East Lane
Spring Valley, NY 10977
(914) 362–5222
e-mail: *info@focusing.org*

The Focusing Institute is a not-for-profit organization that collects and makes resources on focusing available to the academic and professional worlds and to the public. This information is based on Focusing-Oriented Psychotherapy, which teaches clients to turn their vision inward and learn to act from an inner-focused connection.

STOP JUGGLING AND START LIVING

If you obey all the rules you miss all the fun.

KATHARINE HEPBURN

I spend a lot of my time at various conferences, speaking with people in business about issues concerning the balance of work and life. I've had a chance to listen to the challenges faced by employees and business owners alike who are working very hard to succeed, often at the cost of their personal lives.

The way I see it, when it's comes to the balance between work and life, there's good news and there's bad news. The good news is that companies are starting to look at how performance and effectiveness are affected by the lack of such a balance. And people are getting fed up with having to choose between the two. The bad news is that it's only the beginning, and many bright hard-working people continue to suffer in silence, struggling to keep many balls in the air.

At the risk of sounding dramatic, it's important to remember that when we put the needs of our business or company before our personal lives, we put our lives at risk. Not only do we put our emotional and physical health in jeopardy, we put our relationships with loved ones at risk as well. And of course, we damage the most important relationship of all — our relationship to ourselves.

There is an old joke that says, "I've never heard a résumé read at a funeral." Funny as it may sound, it's a line I always remember, because it drives home an important point. It's unlikely that your boss will be at your bedside at the end of your life, thanking you for working so hard or for not taking vacations. Or that clients or customers will be talking about how great you were for missing those family events in order to take care of their needs. The only thing that will matter at the end of your life is how much you loved and were loved by others and what kind of legacy you'll leave behind. The most important person you'll need to answer to is you.

There is a connection between our personal happiness and our ability to be successful at work. For example, when we neglect our health, we get sick and end up taking time off. When we have trouble with or neglect our relationships, we become worried about the problems at home, and as a result we become far less effective at the office. And when we feel overwhelmed and distracted by too much work, we increase our chances of making mistakes. These are just a few examples of how neglecting our personal needs can negatively impact our work.

I could focus this week's chapter on how you'll need to delegate better, manage your time more efficiently, or get your priorities straight to create more balance; but it's clear that going there would be dealing with the symptoms and not the source of the problem. Dealing with the source is an inside job.

To become more productive and effective at work *while* enjoying a fulfilling personal life, you'll have to give up the juggling act and let a few balls drop. Here are some of the balls I'd recommend you let go of first:

Trying to please everyone

Trying to have everyone like you

Trying to be a star at the expense of your life

Trying to do everything perfectly

Trying to do everything

Your reliance on adrenaline

Now I can hear some of you saying, "Sure, easy for you to say, but I have a boss to answer to," or, "I don't have the luxury of letting go, I've got a family to feed." But by now, most of us realize that working like crazy isn't working. Start slowly and let the change begin inside of you. Be willing to break a few rules in order to reclaim your life. As you change your behavior, you'll not only become more effective at work, you'll also become a powerful example for others—the kind of example that leaders are made of.

TAKE ACTION CHALLENGE

This week, as you consider the balls you may be juggling, ask yourself how you'll need to grow in order to let one drop. Pick one item from the list above and notice where it plays out in your daily life. If you're a people pleaser, challenge yourself to say no at least once a day to something you normally would have said yes to. If you're trying to do everything, let your boss know that you've got too many priorities and ask him or her to help you make a choice. If you're not sure how to make a change, ask someone you trust for three specific ideas and request their support. Remember: your life is worth it!

The first ball I'd like to drop is:

_____

The way it plays out in my life is:

_____

The new behavior I will practice this week is:

_____

RESOURCES

The Artist's Way at Work by Mark
Bryan with Julia Cameron and
Catherine Allen (New York:
William Morrow, 1998)

Adapting their techniques for fostering creativity as a means to
spiritual fulfillment for the workplace, the authors show that people can thrive at their jobs when
they take time to nurture their
spirit and listen to their thoughts.

***Creating the Work You Love:
Courage, Commitment and Career***
by Rick Jarow (audio program)
To order:
Sounds True
413 S. Arthur Avenue
Louisville, CO 80027
(800) 333–9185

In this unique and provocative
look at work, career counselor
Rick Jarow argues for a return to
the concept of vocation—finding a
"calling" instead of a job.

Codependent No More, by Melody
Beattie (Hazelden, 1996)

This book will show you how to
stop controlling others and start
caring for yourself.

***Chicken Soup for the Soul at Work:
101 Stories of Courage, Compassion and Creativity in the Workplace*** by Jack Canfield, Mark
Victor Hansen, Martin Rutte,
Maida Rogerson, and Tim Clauss
(Florida: Health Communications,
1996)

Employees and employers alike
will savor these soul-strengthening
accounts of individuals who discover spiritual values and find personal fulfillment on the job.

A Real Life
245 8th Avenue, PMB 400
New York, NY 10011
(802) 893–7040

A Real Life is a newsletter that helps
readers make better choices in
their lives. Subscription: $30 for 6
issues per year.

CHECK UNDER
THE HOOD

*What lies behind us and what lies before us are tiny
matters compared to what lies within us.*

RALPH WALDO EMERSON

When we want to visit a distant place we've never been to before, we often follow a simple plan of action. We choose a destination, create a map, check under the hood, and drive onward until we arrive at our desired location. If we do our planning well, we can even estimate our time of arrival pretty accurately.

We go through this same sort of ritual when we want to accomplish a goal. We clarify the goal (our destination). We create a plan of action (our map). And we take action consistently, hoping to arrive at our desired location pretty quickly. There's only one problem—we usually forget to check under the hood.

Have you ever wondered why a certain goal never gets accomplished? You put a great strategy in place. You take action consistently. You get close. But no matter how hard you try, there always seems to be something that gets in your way of success. The divine, in its infinite wisdom, has perfect timing. When things don't go the way we plan, we could very well be receiving a message to wait, or, to head in a different direction. But there are those times when intuitively we know that there's more to it than that. We feel stuck, and we may even begin to wonder if a "fear of success" or "fear of failure" may be the culprit.

This is when it's time to look inside — under the hood. Too often when embarking on a journey, we focus on what needs to get done without looking at *who* we need to become in order to get there. For example, if you want to publish a book, you'll need to develop the ability to delay gratification. Or if you want to become a successful investment broker, you'll need to develop impeccable communication skills in order to build trust and rapport with your clients. Knowledge and information are never enough.

How do *you* need to grow in order to achieve your goal? Is there a quality that you need to develop, like patience or empathy; an inner muscle that needs to be strengthened? These are important questions to ask yourself when you feel stuck or, better yet, before embarking on any project or goal. To learn more about how to identify the quality you might need to develop more strongly within yourself, get to work on this week's Take Action Challenge. Once you've checked under the hood and made the right adjustments, you'll probably find that you reach your destination with much more joy and ease.

TAKE ACTION CHALLENGE

To discover how you might need to develop yourself in order to fulfill your goal, try this four-step process:

1. Identify someone who is doing what you'd like to do (make sure that person is *very* successful).

2. List three qualities that contribute to this person's success.

3. Pick the one quality you know you need to develop most of all. (Often it's the one that causes you to feel excited and scared at the same time.)

4. Look for practical ways to develop this quality every day.

Example:

Let's imagine that your goal is to become a well-known talk-show host. You identify Oprah Winfrey as your favorite example of success. As you consider her top three qualities, you list:

1. Courage — boldness of action

2. Vulnerability — the ability to easily share herself with others

3. Risk taking — a willingness to venture into the unknown

When you consider this list, you realize that the quality you need to develop most of all is courage. So, each day you do something bold. You swing out and take chances. Maybe you get a completely new hairstyle (one you've dreamt about for a long, long time) or finally end a relationship that drains your energy. If you take practical actions *every day* to develop this part of your character, you'll not only arrive at your destination much sooner, you'll also enjoy a smoother ride.

One person I admire is:

_____

The three qualities I admire most are:

1. _____

2. _____

3. _____

The one quality I need to develop is:

_____

To develop this quality, I will take the following three actions:

1. _____

2. _____

3. _____

RESOURCES

Reinventing Yourself by Steve Chandler (Career Press, September 1998)

This is a great resource for learning how to become the person you've always wanted to be.

The Path of Least Resistance: **Learning to Become the Creative Force in Your Own Life** by Robert Fritz (New York: Fawcett Books, 1989)

A revolutionary program for creating anything, from a functional kitchen to a computer program to a work of art, using your innate power to create.

GIVE YOUR BRAIN A VACATION

Our brightest blazes of gladness are commonly kindled by unexpected sparks.

SAMUEL JOHNSON

Have you ever wondered why you get some of your best ideas in the shower? Or, why you become more and more insightful as each day of your vacation passes by? It all has to do with how you think.

There are two basic modes of operation for the human brain. There is the analytical, thinking mode — the mode we use when we want to memorize something, review financial reports, or learn a new skill. And, there is the relaxed, insightful mode — the one that allows us to rest our thoughts, be present in the moment, and access wisdom. This is the mode we shift to when taking a shower or while relaxing on vacation. Both modes are important, and each can be more useful when used in the right way.

Because our culture is so overly-focused on information, most of us live from the neck up. We spend so much time thinking, analyzing, and trying to figure things out that our brains stay stuck in this analytical mode of operation. When we stay stuck in this mode, we're usually worrying about the past or the future, and this mental focus seriously compromises the quality of our lives in the present moment. For example, if you worry about the meeting you have with your boss at the end of the week, ruminating about what might happen, this kind of analytical thinking can ruin the rest of your week. Or if you're suffering over how to solve a problem and your mind seems to be going around in circles without a solution in sight, there's a pretty good chance that your brain is stuck in an intellectual loop.

There is nothing wrong with the analytical mode of thinking. But when we rely on the analytical, computing mode to handle situations of a less definitive nature (like creative writing, solving problems or relating to others), we end up struggling to "figure things out" rather than allowing the answer to surface effortlessly. Let me give you an example of what I mean.

When I was writing my first book, I learned to use my relaxed brain to make the process more joyful. As I was about to begin a new chapter (usually the most difficult part for me), I would ask my brain to begin working on an outline and to have it ready by 3 P.M. Then I'd go to the beach with a good book and spend the early afternoon relaxing in the sun. Each time my mind started thinking about the chapter I needed to write (analytical mode), I simply told myself, "It's being handled." Then I'd go back to relaxing (insightful mode). Sure enough, when I returned to my computer at 3 P.M., the chapter would start to pour out. Actually, in the beginning, it dripped out. But as I grew to trust the process of letting go and letting my insightful mind take over, the writing flowed more easily. That's what happens when you give your brain a vacation—you access wisdom in a much easier way.

If you want to enjoy life more fully, the trick is to teach yourself to live in the insightful mode more often. That way you'll have more of the analytical brain available for other "stuff"—like putting the gas grill together this summer.

TAKE ACTION CHALLENGE

This week I'd like you to try an experiment. Pick a problem or challenge, and instead of ruminating over and over in your mind about what should be done, ask your relaxed brain to solve the problem while you do something else. Set a specific time for the answer to surface and let it go. Create your own mantra to use when your analytical brain tries to take over, and when you're ready, arrive at the intended result time and see what shows up.

Practicing this simple exercise on a regular basis will not only teach you to access your inner wisdom, but it will also train your brain to use this mode of thinking more often. Once you learn to spend more time in the relaxed mode, you'll find that your imagination runs wild and your ability to access wisdom happens in a snap.

The problem/challenge or idea that I'll practice with this week is:

_____

When my analytical brain kicks in, I will simply say:

_____

I'll check back in for answers on _____ at _____.

RESOURCES

Slowing Down to the Speed of Life
by Richard Carlson and Joseph V.
Bailey (San Francisco, California:
Harper, March 2000)

A simple and powerful guide to
creating a peaceful life from the
inside out.

*Connecting to Creativity: Ten Keys
to Unlocking Your Creative Potential* by Elizabeth W. Bergmann
and Elizabeth O. Colton (Sterling,
Virginia: Capital Books, 1999)

*Sanctuaries the Complete United
States: A Guide to Lodgings in
Monasteries, Abbeys, and Retreats*
by Jack Kelly and Marcia Kelly
(New York: Bell Tower, 1996)

If you'd like to find a quiet place to
rest, you might check out this
book. All of the featured places
welcome people of every denomi-
nation. Most are Christian, but
many are Buddhist, Sufi, and
Hindu, and a few have no specific
religious ties.

*Inspiration Sandwich: Stories to
Inspire Our Creative Freedom* by
Sark (California: Celestial Arts,
1992)

When you're looking for a little fun
and inspiration, Sark's books can
be fun companions.

*Capture the Rapture: How to Step
Out of Your Head and Leap Into
Life* by Marcia Reynolds (Hathor
Hill Press, 2000)
To order:
Covisioning
P.O. Box 5012
Scottsdale, AZ 85261
(888) 998–5064

Learn how to revive your passion
and find the joy available in every
moment of your life.

SPRING INTO FITNESS

*I like to exercise, but it's not always possible with
my hectic sleep schedule.*

UNKNOWN

Springtime is usually the time of year that many of us start
to think about getting in shape, and so I've turned to the
wisest person I know for some fitness advice—my husband Michael Gerrish. Michael is a fitness professional who has
not only dedicated his life to helping people find their unique fitness formula, but he's also "walked the talk" from the age of
ten. As an exercise physiologist, Michael began to notice that
emotion-life issues were consistently undermining his clients'
success. Inspired by this realization, he went on to get his mas-
ters degree in counseling psychology. Since then Michael has
expanded his study of emotional and physical fitness to include
the energetic blocks that prevent people from leading healthy
lives.

Creating a healthy lifestyle is a holistic process. While most
of us know that this process involves improving our body and
mind, research has revealed other areas that should be con-
sidered as well. One such area involves what are referred to as
energy fields and the ways imbalances in these fields can affect
the ways we feel, perform, and think. Some of the therapies used
to correct these imbalances are Thought-Field Therapy (TFT)
and Emotional Freedom Techniques (EFT). Through his work

Michael has found that these energy fields and/or pathways (similar to those affected by acupuncture) are often blocked in ways that prevent us from following through with, or benefiting from, our efforts to lose weight or get in shape.

Time and again Michael has found that blocks or disruptions in these fields can restrict our energy, decrease or sabotage our motivation, and ultimately set us up to fail. As a result of studying this new field, Michael began using TFT and other energy therapies in his work with clients and has seen a marked increase in the rate of their success. There is amazing research emerging in this field, and I've provided additional information in the resource section at the end of this chapter.

I'd like to share the eight most important things I've learned from Michael about creating a healthy lifestyle, in the hopes that it supports you in your quest for a healthier body, mind, and spirit.

1. There's more to getting fit than eating well and regular exercise. Getting fit is an emotional, spiritual, psychological, and physical process. If you do not consider all four areas in your fitness plan, the chances of failure are pretty high.

In addition to this holistic approach, there are obstacles that can prevent even the most well-meaning people from succeeding. These obstacles can be things like food allergies, depression, hormone imbalances, ADD, underactive thyroid, and more. If you are unaware of your obstacles, chances are that you'll continue to beat yourself up when you fail. I've included information on how to identify and overcome your obstacles in the resource section at the end of this chapter.

2. When you shift your focus from losing weight to creating a daily practice of self-care, your chances of long-term success increase dramatically. Although weight loss may be important to you, let that be a byproduct of living a healthy lifestyle.

3. There are no "one size fits all" eating and exercise plans. Learn to eat well for your body type and find the form of exercise that best suits your individual needs and desires.

4. You don't need to lose a certain amount of weight to feel good about yourself. You only need to take good care of your body *today*. When I used to feel frustrated by how long it might take me to reach my goal weight, Michael would remind me to focus "just for today" on eating well and exercising. By doing this, I eliminated the biggest obstacle to getting and staying in shape—negative self talk.

5. Take a break from the catalog and magazine subscriptions that contain air-brushed, computer-enhanced images, they only create self-loathing. When you look at the photos and start to think, "If only I had that body" or, "I'll never look like that," you're headed for a downward spiral that will almost certainly send you to the refrigerator and/or the couch.

6. Engaging in a simple, appropriate free-weight program is a powerful way to reconnect with your body and burn fat. When I first watched Michael work out, I witnessed for the first time weight training as a form of meditation. As he taught me to focus and move slowly, putting my full attention on the muscle I was strengthening, I connected to my body in a deeper, more spiritual way. Surprisingly, learning to exercise in a slower, more deliberate fashion allowed me to achieve much better results in significantly less time.

7. You will fall off the fitness path throughout your life—that's a given. But when you do, always remember that getting back on track *and* feeling good about yourself is just one healthy food choice or one workout away.

8. Finally, the most important advice of all: it's okay to give yourself a break. An occasional ice-cream sundae or a missed week of exercise won't kill you. The quest for perfection, on the other hand, probably will.

TAKE ACTION CHALLENGE

This week consider the obstacles that might prevent you from achieving your fitness goals. For example, you might not be a morning person and yet you keep expecting yourself to get up earlier to go to the gym. Or you might hate using the indoor machines but you don't allow yourself to do something fun outside because you think exercise needs to be hard work. Other obstacles might include certain foods like caffeine or sugar, an injury that might prevent you from working out, and a busy schedule.

In the spaces below, list five obstacles that might prevent you from creating a healthy lifestyle. Then, next to each obstacle, list a possible solution that will help you to overcome the obstacle so you can move toward positive change. For example, if you have an injury, make an appointment with a professional to have it checked out. Or switch from coffee with caffeine to decaf.

Once you've listed the five obstacles and solutions, choose one solution and implement the change this week. It only takes one small action over time to produce results.

OBSTACLES   SOLUTIONS

1. _____   1. _____

2. _____   2. _____

3. _____   3. _____

4. _____   4. _____

5. _____   5. _____

RESOURCES

When Working Out Isn't Working Out: **A Mind/Body Guide to Conquering Unidentified Fitness Obstacles (UFOs)** by Michael Gerrish (New York: St. Martin's Griffin, 1999)

This groundbreaking book is a comprehensive guide to identifying and overcoming hidden blocks that may be preventing you from becoming optimally fit. For more info visit Gerrish's Web site at: *www.exerciseplus.com*

The Mind-Body Makeover Project by Michael Gerrish (McGraw-Hill Contemporary, 2003)

Women's Bodies, Women's Wisdom by Christiane Northrup, M.D. (New York: Bantam Doubleday Dell, March 1998)

This book is an excellent resource on women's health from a holistic perspective.

www.eNUTRITION.com

A Web site full of health products, information, and inspiration to help you achieve your health goals.

www.OnHealth.com

OnHealth is a compilation of the best national and international resources to give you the most reliable information on the topics you choose in the world of health and wellness.

The Courage to Start: A Guide to Running for your Life by John Bingham (New York: Simon & Schuster/Fireside, 1999)

A funny and inspirational guide for beginning runners.

For more information on Thought Field Therapy contact:
Roger Callahan
Callahan Techniques
78-816 Via Carmel
La Quinta, CA 92253
(800) 359–CURE (2873)
http://www.tftrx.com

This is the Web site for the founder of this unique and amazing energy therapy that helps cure everything from phobias to addictions and more.

Instant Emotional Healing by Peter Lambrou and George Pratt (New York: Broadway Books, 2000)

Two leading clinical psychologists offer a revolutionary new method using thought field therapy for ridding yourself of everything from stress, claustrophobia, procrastination, jet lag, rejection, and more.

ARE WE HAVING FUN YET?

Life is not a stress rehearsal

LORETTA LAROCHE

When's the last time you had fun? A good long belly laugh or a thrilling experience that made you catch your breath? You know, the kind of activity that keeps a smile on your face for at least thirty minutes? Sound vaguely familiar? I don't know about you, but I can take life so seriously sometimes that I get involved in a project or the pursuit of a goal, delve deeply, and rarely come up for air. As a matter of fact, I always know when fun is missing from my daily diet when the very mention of the word annoys me.

Fun is a vital nutrient for a high-quality life, and for most of us this nutrient is in short supply. Wouldn't it be great if we could buy "fun powder" at the local health-food store, much like a protein drink, and mix up a serving before heading off to work? Until then you'll have to work a little harder to make fun a part of your daily diet.

Doing something out of the ordinary can be a great way to add some fun to your life. Try something you haven't done in a while. Go sledding with the kids (or grab the neighbor's kids if you don't have any—with the parents' permission, of course). Take an afternoon off and see a funny movie. Go dancing with a friend. Or keep a funny tape in your car so that you can enjoy a good laugh while driving to work.

Life is short. Life is too busy. Life can be a pain in the butt sometimes. The remedy: a dose of fun, at least once a day, should do the trick!

TAKE ACTION CHALLENGE

Stop right now, open your word processor, and make a sign (using at least 24 point font) that says: AM I HAVING FUN YET? Print this sign and hang it in your home or office. Use it to remind yourself to do something fun at least two times this week. (Remember the 30-minute smile test!)

For those of you who forget how to have fun, don't worry. Anticipating this problem, I consulted some "fun experts" for a top-ten list (my nieces and nephews, ranging in ages from three to eight). Here's what they came up with:

1. Play with your friends.

2. Try video games (and don't worry if you're not good at first).

3. Go to the toy store.

4. Hold a kitten.

5. Eat an ice cream (a BIG one, 'cause it lasts longer).

6. Slide down a slide or swing on the swings.

7. Go to the beach and splash a lot.

8. Go sledding and take your mittens.

9. Play at the gym (a jungle gym).

10. Don't take a shower.

The three things I'd like to do for fun are:

1. _____

2. _____

3. _____

RESOURCES

Relax — You May Only Have a Few Minutes Left by Loretta LaRoche (New York: Villard Books, 1998)

Using the power of humor to overcome stress in your life and work.

Loretta LaRoche — Humor Potential Inc.
(800) 99–Tadah
www.lorettalaroche.com

This Web site offers videos, audio programs, products, and books related to humor and destressing.

Camp SARK
(415) 546–3742
www.campsark.com/campsark/swwgroups.html

Visit this site to learn how to hold your own Succulent Wild Woman Group or Party – a great way to connect with other succulent souls!

Outward Bound
www.outwardbound.com
(888) 882–6863

Not just for kids! Outward Bound is not just a wilderness adventure, it's also a personal experience — you will challenge self-imposed limits, try new things, and develop new attitudes and approaches.

TWO HEADS RUN BETTER THAN ONE

Partnerships are the intentional co-mingling of talents and energies, the giving of all each partner has to offer, for the reaching of a common goal and the mutual benefit of all concerned. Partnering is the future of all soulful endeavors.

STACY BRICE

Not long ago I had the pleasure (and challenge) of running in my first road race with my sister Lisa. Our goal was to finish the race without walking. When we arrived on Saturday morning, in the midst of 10–20 mph winds and 35 degrees, we were surprised to discover several steep hills covering half the distance of the course. As we stood staring at the crest of the first hill just beyond the starting line, we began to get nervous; for some reason we had both assumed that the course would be flat and easy (ah, you know what they say about assumptions).

Running the race together reminded me about the power of partnership. Although there were several times when I wanted to stop and walk, Lisa's encouragement and presence kept me going. We were a team, and having her by my side made it impossible to give up or give in to the little voice in my head that said I couldn't make it through. Our energy together was far stronger than our energy alone, and there were times when I could actually feel myself being pulled forward by Lisa's momentum.

Partnership can be a powerful prescription for any situation. The emotional roller-coaster ride of living through a divorce or serious illness can be handled much more easily with the comfort and support of someone at your side. Or the completion of an important goal, like finishing school or planning a wedding, becomes less overwhelming with a partner to share in the work. Sometimes a friend simply makes a daunting task of moving or cleaning out the basement more bearable.

Too often we neglect to ask for help. Conditioned to go it alone, we may fear appearing weak or needy. And for many of us, it simply doesn't occur to us to reach out to others for support. But partnership can have an amazing impact on the lives of each person involved.

I still remember the time when I finally asked for help and hired my first assistant, Stacy Brice. What started out as administrative support quickly became a partnership that not only took my business to a whole new level but launched a new profession as well. Within a week I found myself wondering why I had waited so long to ask for help, and at the end of the first year my business had far exceeded my goals. And this partnership not only changed my life; it changed Stacy's life, too.

As a result of our virtual arrangement, Stacy went on to launch a whole new profession based on partnership called "virtual assisting." She created a virtual university called "Assist U" that provides training to "virtual assistants" wanting to partner with business owners. And not only that, her organization provides a free referral service that connects business owners with great assistants as well! That's what partnership does—it creates something much bigger than the two people involved.

Human beings are not meant to live in isolation. Sharing ourselves in partnership with another deepens our connection and gives us the courage and strength to move beyond our limitations. Best of all, taking a partner along for the ride means sharing in the celebration of your success. For me that was the best part of the race with my sister. As Lisa and I approached the finish line, I'm sure we looked pretty silly yelling and screaming like two little kids, *but* we were definitely having fun!

TAKE ACTION CHALLENGE

This week pick a goal or project and find a partner. For example, you might ask a coworker to walk with you during lunchtime so that you can support each other as you get in shape. Or you and a friend might each choose a project that you've been putting off and challenge each other to finish it by the end of the week. Maybe it's time for you to hire an assistant or support person too? Whether it's the simple act of speaking with someone before and after a difficult phone call or the more challenging task of getting help with your taxes, give yourself (and someone else) the chance to experience the power of partnership firsthand!

The project I'd like support with is:

_____

Three potential partners are:

1. _____

2. _____

3. _____

RESOURCES

Assist U
(410) 666–5900
http://www.assistu.com

This organization offers training for virtual assistants and a referral service for qualified VAs.

Dance Lessons : Six Steps to Great Partnerships in Business & Life by Chip R. Bell and Heather Shea (Berrett-Koehler, 1998)

A step-by-step guide to managing the personal side of business partnerships.

STOP, LOOK, AND LISTEN

When you find yourself declaring that absolutely, no way, can you possibly take time off, that is exactly when you need to.

JENNIFER LOUDEN

N ow that you've been making changes over the last several weeks, it's the perfect time to reward yourself with a pamper break! If you're like most people, you probably feel overwhelmed, exhausted, and fed up with all there is to do (although you should be feeling better as a result of taking the actions so far). Too often I hear people say that they'll give themselves a break or a chance to relax *once* everything is done. Well, I have news for you:

The In Box of Life Never Empties!

Our fast-paced, adrenaline-based culture will trap you into believing that you'll finally be able to relax once you make that one last phone call, finish one more task, or respond to one more e-mail. But before you know it, you're on overload and your body can't seem to slow down. I've been fooled by this myth too, and because of that, I've trained myself to *Stop, Look,* and *Listen.*

It's during the busiest times, when we're the most stressed

out, that we need to *Stop* what we're doing, *Look* at our priorities, and *Listen* to our bodies. Although we may be able to push through the challenging period, I can assure you that stress and hardship take their toll. Soon we're hit with the perfect excuse to stop—illness.

Instead of pushing your self-care to the end of your to-do list, learn to build in self-care breaks *during* the most stressful times. Don't wait for illness to stop you. By doing this, you'll become more sensitive to the signals of stress (tight shoulders and neck, anxiety, racing mind, sleep loss, and so on), and you'll take action to handle it *before* it gets too close. Regardless of what's going on in your life right now, give yourself permission to stop and take a pamper break.

TAKE ACTION CHALLENGE

Stop right now and schedule a self-care break. You might try one of the following:

1. Call a family member and ask that person to take the kids for the night (or, even better, the weekend!).

2. Schedule a massage.

3. Call a friend and ask for help.

4. See that movie you've been dying to see.

5. Take a nap during the middle of the day (if you're at work, be sure and lock your door!).

6. Schedule a date night with your partner.

7. Take a long bath or create an at-home spa for an evening.

If you're not sure what form of self-care is best, try answering the following question: What could you do for yourself this week that would make you feel guilty? As long as the answer doesn't hurt you or anyone else, go for it!

This week, my self-care gift will be:

_____

RESOURCES

**National Certification Board
for Therapeutic Massage &
Bodywork (NCBTMB)**
8201 Greensboro Drive, Suite 300,
McLean, VA 22102
(800) 296–0664 *(totally automated
line)*
www.ncbtmb.com

A resource for publications, area practitioners, and consumer guide information.

The Comfort Queen's Guide to Life
by Jennifer Louden (New York:
Harmony Books, 2000)

In this beautifully illustrated spiritual organizer, Jennifer Louden helps women create their lives from the inside out by helping them to find their own Comfort Queen within.

Spa Finders
www.spafinders.com

If you are looking for guidance on choosing a spa resort, this is a good place to start.

Omega Institute
260 Lake Drive
Rhinebeck, NY 12572
(800) 944–1001
www.eomega.org

The country's largest alternative education and retreat center. It is an oasis for people aspiring to know and heal themselves and to mingle with others on the same search.

**American Red Cross Babysitter's
Training Course**
www.redcross.org

A great resource for parents who want to find a trained baby-sitter. This twelve-hour course is offered through local Red Cross chapters nationally. It is designed for eleven-to-fifteen-year-olds and includes a *Babysitter's Handbook* and first-aid kit.

Rod Stryker's meditation CD
To order:
www.pureyoga.com
(888) 398–9642

A wonderful CD that takes the listener through a simple step-by-step process that teaches you how to meditate with ease.

Meditations for Healing Stress
(audiocassette) by Susie Levan, music by Steven Halpern
Susie Levan
P.O. Box 8608
Ft. Lauderdale, FL 33310–8608
(954) 382–4325

A calm, guided visualization tape that will help you to eliminate stress.

Shower Posters: Questions to reflect upon while enjoying a shower.
To order:
Power Questions
5430 Glen Lakes, Suite 240
Dallas, TX 75231
(800) 503–9920
www.powerquestions.com

Take a moment to reflect on thoughts that over time will help guide you on a path to more conscious living. They make unique, inexpensive gifts too!

CREATING SPACE

Out of clutter, find simplicity.

ALBERT EINSTEIN

I am a stickler for creating space. Not that I'm obsessive about it (although I bet my husband would disagree), I just need plenty of room to think, relax, create, and breathe. It's taken me about five years to train myself to eliminate clutter and excess from its source. It's become a simple ritual: when in doubt, throw it out. Learning to eliminate clutter at its source deals with the problem at the root level. For example, weeding through your mail *when* you receive it, and throwing away as much as you can, helps stop the flow of paper before it gets to your desk, your to-do pile, or the infamous junk drawer. Going through your current to-do pile with a mind-set of letting go of those "maybe I'll do this someday" kind of projects can be another great way to nip future clutter in the bud.

Teaching yourself to eliminate clutter is an important life skill to develop, especially in our overloaded "information age." Too many of us have become reliant on information. We save magazines, catalogs, old records, even outdated textbooks. And we keep stacks of paper around because we're afraid that we just might need something in them someday. It's not that information is bad—we need information to help us make informed decisions. But our overreliance on external information puts us in the habit of constantly looking outside of ourselves for the answers instead of using another key resource—our gut instinct or intuition—the place where wisdom resides.

Anything you've ever wanted to know about everything is now available on the Web. If you don't believe me, go to a search engine and type in a word. Notice how much information shows up (toothpaste: 28,000 entries; leadership consulting: 819). Why not use the Web to your advantage and free yourself from clutter and piles?

Creating space makes you feel better physically and emotionally. Once you've eliminated those things that have been draining your energy, you can actually feel the energy move back into your body. And when that happens, your mind clears and your mood lifts as well. Let's try a little experiment. Stop right now and look around the room. Is there an area that needs to be freed from clutter? An overflowing wastebasket or a bookcase stacked with piles? How long have you been meaning to clear that area up? Notice what happens in your body *and* in your mind when you focus on that space.

If you're like most people, you've probably been meaning to get to that clutter for a while, and the combination of negative self-talk and visual mess drains your energy. When we finally get around to clearing it up, we always feel more energized and motivated. (Don't worry, you'll get to experience this soon).

Okay, enough convincing. Let's get started. See the Take Action Challenge below and repeat after me: when in doubt, throw it out; when in doubt, throw it out; when in doubt, throw it out. . . .

TAKE ACTION CHALLENGE

Here's the deal. This week pick one area that could use some cleaning out and challenge yourself to throw away *more* than feels comfortable. Take an hour during the afternoon to pull out a filing-cabinet drawer and weed out old files. Tackle a closet that's been driving you nuts. Clean off the hard drive on your computer. Or attack that junk drawer you've been meaning to get to. Think of this exercise as developing a new twenty-first-century life skill. Letting go of more than you feel comfortable with is less about clearing the clutter and more about training yourself to develop a "when in doubt, throw it out" mentality. This mentality deals with the source of the problem.

When you're done, sit in front of the cleared space for at least five minutes and notice how you feel. The combination of feeling relaxed and energized at the same time is what creating space is all about.

RESOURCES

Merry Maids
(800) 637–7962
www.merrymaids.com

Nationwide cleaning service. Call their toll-free number or visit the Web site for information.

Garage/Yard Sales . . . A Great Way to Make Extra Money! by Carol A. Bland, editor (Kansas: Wyandotte West Communications, 1998)

A small booklet putting garage-sale tips, hints, strategies, and ideas all in one easy-to-read place.

www.zerojunkmail.com
(888) 970–5865

This service is dedicated to helping consumers rid their lives of unwanted junk mail, including e-mail, as well as unwanted phone calls from telemarketers.

National Association of Professional Organizers (NAPO)
1033 La Posada, Suite 220
Austin, TX 78752
Referral Line: (512) 206–0151
Web site address: *www.napo.net*

This organization can help with referrals to a Professional Organizer in your area.

Organizing From the Inside Out by Julie Morganstern (Owl Books, September 1998)

The foolproof system for organizing your home, your office, and your life.

A Housekeeper Is Cheaper Than a Divorce by Kathy Fitzgerald Sherman (California: Life Tools Press, 2000)

Why you can afford to hire help and how to get it.

Home Comforts by Cheryl Mendelson (New York: Scribner, 1999)

The book guides readers through every challenge they will face: guilt feelings, tax mysteries, language barriers, training challenges, quality standards, and finding the perfect person to handle your daily drudgery.

Clear Your Clutter with Feng Shui by Karen Kingston (New York: Broadway Books, May 1999)

A wonderful introduction to the concepts of feng shui and a very valid argument of how clutter can negatively impact your life.

FOCUS YOUR ENERGY

*To bring one's self to a frame of mind and to the proper
energy to accomplish things that require plain hard work
continuously is the one big battle that everyone has. When
this battle is won for all time, then everything is easy.*

THOMAS A. BUCKNER

Life is so funny. When I had decided to title this chapter "Focus Your Energy" and to write about the importance of setting priorities and eliminating distractions as an aid to getting focused, I found one morning, as I lay in bed thinking about the points I wanted to make, that several more ideas for other chapters flooded my mind. As I started to consider the various topics, I began to feel antsy and a bit overwhelmed. Then it dawned on me: I was letting these other ideas distract me from my focus.

So, back to the original plan . . .

If you've ever felt pulled in too many directions at once, you've probably experienced the frustration and discomfort of what I call "splattered energy." Splattered energy is what occurs when our attention is distracted and we're pulled off center. I'm sure you've experienced this before: You're focused on writing an important e-mail, the phone rings, you lose your train of thought, and your mind is off and running to other things. Or you're reading a report for an important meeting, someone enters your office, and you completely forget everything you've just read. These kinds of distractions not only waste precious time, they waste precious energy as well. And, they cause us to feel frustrated, anxious, and eventually overwhelmed.

In our modern day of voice mail, e-mail, faxes, and cell phones, it's no wonder we have such a hard time focusing our energy on what really matters. Too often we allow ourselves to be pulled away from our priorities in order to respond to the needs of someone else. But, if you want to honor your priorities *and* get your work done more effectively, you'll need to gather your splattered energy and refocus your attention.

Here's a little trick I use when I get busy to help make my days more productive and joyful. My most focused and stress-free days happen when I take time in the morning to intentionally set the day's agenda. Before going into my office, I sit quietly and do the following:

1. List my top three priorities for the week in my journal.

2. List the three most important actions I can take today to honor these priorities.

3. Anticipate and eliminate distractions.

Once you know what your priorities are and have identified the actions to support them, don't wait to be distracted. Anticipate the possible distractions and eliminate them *before* they occur. For example, when writing is a priority, I always turn the ringer off on my phone because I know I'm distracted by noise. Or if I've set aside an afternoon to return phone calls, I turn off my computer so that my attention is not pulled away by e-mail.

Let's imagine that your top three priorities for the week are:

1. Exercise

2. Finish a report for work

3. Spend quality time with my family

The three most important actions you might take today are:

1. Schedule three dates this week in my calendar to exercise (in ink).

2. Block out a two-hour period to finish my report.

3. Arrange a family picnic for the weekend.

The potential distractions that you can eliminate ahead of time are:

1. Last minute problems. Complete all work one half-hour before I plan to exercise.

2. Interruptions. Post a DO NOT DISTURB sign on my door at work.

3. Weekend work temptations. Leave all work at my office on Friday, so that I have the weekend completely free to spend with my family.

When you put your priorities and actions *in writing* and start your workday by eliminating any possible distractions, you'll find it much easier to stay focused (and stress-free) throughout the day.

TAKE ACTION CHALLENGE

During this week use the first fifteen minutes of each day to create your own ritual. Find a comfortable place to write and identify your top three priorities for the week. Next, list the actions you'll take to honor these priorities during the day. And finally, challenge yourself to identify at least three possible distractions and eliminate them *before* you start your day.

My top three priorities for the week are:

1. _____

2. _____

3. _____

The five actions I need to take this week to honor these priorities are:

1. _____

2. _____

3. _____

4. _____

5. _____

The possible distractions are:

_____

To eliminate these distractions I will:

_____

RESOURCES

First Things First: To Live, To Love, To Learn, To Leave a Legacy by Stephen R. Covey, A. Roger Merrill, and Rebecca R. Merrill (New York: Simon & Schuster/Fireside, 1996)

This book helps you to identify those things that really matter and deserve your focused attention.

Mastery by George Leonard (New York: Dutton, 1982)
http://www.penguin.com

A little book with a whole lot of wisdom.

BRAKE FOR SPONTANEITY

*The greatest gift that you can give yourself is a little
bit of your own attention.*

ANTHONY J. D'ANGELO

D o you ever feel that life is just one long routine day after another? You wake up, take a shower, brush your teeth, get dressed, head off to work, and blah, blah, blah, blah, blah. Well, if one more day of the "same ol' stuff" makes you feel cranky, it might be time for a spontaneity break.

Now I know that the idea of scheduling a spontaneity break sounds like a contradiction in terms, but when you consider how our society lives and thrives by the clock, it makes sense. Too often we fall into the trap of believing that life will become easier and more meaningful when we get really good at living and acting efficiently. But schedules, clocks, and well-planned time can squash our creative spirit—the part of us that thrives on spontaneous, open-ended time.

I love open-ended time. In other words, I love to have an afternoon or day to myself to do whatever I want, without needing to be anywhere or do anything at any given time. As a matter of fact, I can become pretty tough to live with when my calendar gets too full of scheduled appointments (just ask my husband).

When I have open-ended time, I often stop, close my eyes, and check in with myself to determine what feels right in the moment. Sometimes when I check in, I get a goofy answer like, "Clean out the refrigerator" (pretty weird, I know). At other times I may want to take a nap, go for a jog, visit a bookstore, or just sit and relax.

As creative beings, we all need periods of time to live spontaneously without commitments or distractions. By creating the space to live in the moment, we strengthen the connection to our inner wisdom and give ourselves a much-needed rest from the routine of day-to-day living. So, if the idea of brushing your teeth or getting dressed feels like an overwhelming task, it might be time for a spontaneity break!

TAKE ACTION CHALLENGE

Schedule a spontaneity break this week. Take an afternoon or evening and give yourself the gift of time free from appointments or obligations. Do whatever comes to mind in the moment. During this time stop, check in with your Wise Self, and ask, "What do I *really* want to do right now?" However goofy or simple the answer might be, trust your gut and act!

My spontaneous, open-ended time during this week will be:

_____

RESOURCES

Life, Paint and Passion: Reclaiming the Magic of Spontaneous Expression by Michelle Cassou and Stewart Cubley (New York: J. P. Tarcher, 1996)

Explains how to use the creative process as an important tool for self-discovery, encouraging the reader to embark on inner exploration through the unfettered practice of painting as a means of spontaneous expression.

www.recreation.gov

A great resource to find inexpensive or free recreational opportunities nationwide on government land, including: picnic areas, biking, boating, camping, climbing, cultural or historical sites, fishing, hiking, horseback riding, hunting, winter sports, and water sports.

EARLY WARNING SIGNALS

*When you practice Extreme Self Care, you wrap yourself
in an energy that creates miracles in your life and in the
lives of those around you.*

SHIRLEY ANDERSON

The concept of extreme self-care is the foundation of my work. Practicing extreme self-care means taking exceptionally good care of yourself even when it feels uncomfortable or a little self-indulgent. Experience has taught me that many of us struggle with the idea of making our needs and self-care a priority out of fear that the effort may appear selfish or inappropriate. But in order to be there for others in a healthy way, you must first be there for yourself.

Examples of how to practice extreme self care will always be unique to each individual. Some examples might include:

- Getting a baby-sitter or swapping child care with a friend two times a week instead of once a month.

- Giving yourself permission to change your mind about a commitment you've made, even though the change may disappoint someone.

- Asking someone to stop complaining instead of tolerating the whining in order to be "nice" or polite.

- Not eating junk food.

- Asking for help the moment you need it instead of pushing through the discomfort on your own.

- Allowing yourself to spend a bit more money than you feel you deserve in order to get the right bed, car, home, and so on.

- Getting a massage once a week instead of every other month.

I am always so moved and inspired by the people who immediately take to the idea of extreme self-care. Not only are they open-minded and hungry for the message that a high-quality life starts with a high-quality you, they're committed to doing something about it! The more I do this work, the more I appreciate my first coach, Thomas Leonard, for introducing me to this concept of taking much better care of myself than I felt I deserved. I am convinced that extreme self-care is a powerful medicinal concept, much needed in today's busy world.

Often when I'm traveling a lot giving lectures, audience members (and readers) ask me whether or not I'm able to manage my own self-care while keeping such a busy travel schedule. The honest answer is — usually. The idea of learning to practice extreme self-care on a whole new level as my work reaches more people challenges me. I think of my life as part of my research.

To support my efforts, I have the perfect first-aid kit — a terrific coach who helps me to keep my Absolute Yes list (my top priorities) finely tuned, great friends and colleagues who continue to support my growth, and a loving husband, who has my full permission to step in at any moment with a "self-care" flag.

It's not always easy. There are times when I feel overwhelmed. Days when I'm afraid to step into the shoes I've created. And frequent moments when I long for a quiet home in the woods with a flower garden and a dog. But one of the things that keeps me straight and allows me to do what I love is recognizing my "early warning signals"—the behaviors that spell trouble. Let me give you some examples of what I mean.

I know I'm heading for trouble when:

1. I'm driving without wearing my seat belt.

2. I'm too tired to floss.

3. I get less than eight hours of sleep a night.

4. I run out of bottled water in my office.

5. I'm too busy to exercise.

6. I have trouble focusing during the day.

7. I can't get to water the flowers in my window boxes.

8. I go to bed without washing my face.

9. I forget simple things like how to spell the word "the."

10. I leave my office with a desk that's a mess.

Oh, and

11. I start cursing at inanimate objects.

These are the signals that direct me back to extreme self-care. It's not that my life doesn't get crazy—it does. But the amount of time it takes for me to snap back into extreme self-care mode is less and less. I tolerate far less stress than ever before. When I begin to feel the slightest bit overwhelmed I:

1. Ask for help. Whether I need advice or information, emotional support, or someone to do me a favor, I remember to pick up the phone and make a call. I might call my

coach, a friend, a neighbor, or a relative. I might delegate more work to my assistant or simply talk a problem through with my husband. The point is to remember to ask for help.

2. Reevaluate my priorities. I review my Absolute Yes list and notice where I might be spending energy on things that are not important.

3. Identify what I need to let go of in order to stay focused on what's important, and let it go.

It's a simple formula that works. In addition to using these behaviors, there are several things you can use to create your own extreme self-care first aid kit. They include:

- Your Absolute Yes list

- The name and phone numbers of two or three friends who can support you

- A sign that says, "Stop and Breathe" or "This Moment Is Temporary"

- A pair of walking shoes to remind you to get up and walk away from a problem

- A special pillow when a nap might be in order

- Tissues when you simply need a good cry

We have an instinct for survival, not extreme self-care. It's important to be ever vigilant about the quality of your life. Knowing *your* early warning signals will help you prepare the items you'll need to add to your extreme self-care first-aid kit.

TAKE ACTION CHALLENGE

During the week notice when you start to get edgy, irritable, frustrated, or overwhelmed. What behaviors trigger this reaction? What things do you find yourself forgetting about when you get busy? As you notice these things, write them down and create your own early-warning signal list.

Finish the sentence:
I know I'm headed for trouble when . . .

1. _____

2. _____

3. _____

4. _____

5. _____

6. _____

7. _____

8. _____

9. _____

10. _____

Use these signals to remind you to return your attention to your priorities.

Once you've identified your early-warning signals, list the three things you'll put in place to support your extreme self-care.

1. _____

2. _____

3. _____

RESOURCES

The Portable Coach: 28 Surefire Strategies for Business and Personal Success by Thomas J. Leonard (New York: Scribner, August 1998)

This coaching guide will introduce you to revolutionary new ways to make your self-care a top priority in all aspects of your life.

Self-Nurture: Learning to Care for Yourself as Effectively as You Care for Everyone Else by Alice D. Domar and Henry Dreher (New York: Viking, 1999)

This book is a comprehensive year-long program to help readers learn the crucial art of self-nurturing.

O Magazine
The Oprah Magazine
P.O. Box 7831
Red Oak, IA 51591
www.oprah.com

An amazing personal growth magazine for women focused on self-care and personal growth.

LEARNING TO WAIT

I hope you'll hear what I'm about to tell you. I hope you'll hear it all the way down to your toes. When you're waiting, you're not doing nothing. You're doing the most important something there is. You're allowing your soul to grow up. If you can't be still and wait, you can't become what God created you to be.

SUE MONK KIDD, *WHEN THE HEART WAITS*

Have you ever felt frustrated or discouraged while waiting for something you really wanted? A relationship to blossom? Your business to take off? A new baby to come into your life? Maybe you've been forced to wait because you're unsure of what's next, feeling as though your life has fallen victim to a giant hold button.

I have never been a big fan of waiting. Like many, I usually want everything yesterday. And yet, as I look back over my life, the times I've spent waiting have been some of the most meaningful and insightful times of my life. Usually a waiting period has signaled a turning point—a period of soul growth that leads to something better. And, it's during these times of transition that I've settled more deeply into myself, connecting to a strength of character that I hadn't known existed.

Although waiting can feel like agony, it may be exactly what you need to *do* to prepare for the next stage of *your* life. Think of it as a time to connect with your inner wisdom on a whole new level, an opportunity to get to know yourself even better. During a waiting period you might spend more time writing in your journal, invest in your emotional and physical health, pound pillows, or yell and scream. Do what's necessary to embrace the discomfort, knowing that if you use this time wisely, you will strengthen your personal power, the kind of power that no outside person or thing can ever give you.

And remember, although waiting is a personal journey, there is no need to wait in isolation. Share your fears, concerns, and frustrations with trusted loved ones who can support you in your waiting. By doing this, you'll experience another benefit of waiting—a deeper connection to those you love.

TAKE ACTION CHALLENGE

Embrace your time of waiting. If there is an area of your life that feels as though it's on hold, consciously decide to sit with the waiting this week. Don't try to change things, push the flow, or control the circumstances. Instead, sit quietly and be open to the messages from within. Use this time to relax and rest. When the time is right and you're ready to move on, you'll be glad you did.

Just wait . . .

RESOURCES

When the Heart Waits by Sue Monk Kidd (New York: HarperCollins, March 2000)

This book is a must-read for anyone going through transitions and trying to stay spiritually centered and connected.

Contemplative Living by Joan Duncan Oliver (New York: Dell Books, 2000)

One of the best resources I've read on the various ways that we can find peace and comfort in stillness.

A Guide to Monastic Guest Houses by Robert J. Regalbuto (Harrisburg, Pennsylvania: Morehouse, 1998)

Now in its third edition, this book is expanded to offer detailed information on accommodations in every state across the United States and every Canadian province. Illustrations, descriptions, histories, directions, costs, and maps are provided.

Transitions by Julia Cameron (New York: J. P. Tarcher, 1999)

Prayers and declarations for a changing life.

FRIENDS, FACTS, AND FAITH

*I've been absolutely terrified every moment of my life and
I've never let it keep me from doing a single thing that I
wanted to do.*

GEORGIA O'KEEFFE

What's the one thing you know you need to do to improve the quality of your life right now that you're most afraid of doing? For many of us fear is a constant companion on the path of personal change. Fear of the unknown. Fear of the action or reaction of others. Fear of pain or humiliation. Fear of loss. In order for any of us to create a great life, we must confront our fears on a regular basis—it's just a normal part of the human experience. What you do with your fear, however, will direct the course of your life. If you let fear stop you, you'll keep wishing and hoping for a better life.

Fear can be a call to action, a powerful motivating force for change. Although fear can provide a warning of danger, I'm talking about the kind of fear that shows up when you're about to take an action that you know, on a gut level, is important for your growth or the advancement of your goals. The better you get at handling fear, the more amazing your life will become.

In my work as a coach, and as a woman who challenges herself to do scary things on a regular basis, I've learned quite a bit about handling fear. I've realized that with the following three things in place, I can overcome just about anything:

1. *Friends.* Too many of us try to do scary things alone. As far as I'm concerned, that's the old model of "I don't need anyone," and it no longer works (not that it ever worked very well before). Doing scary things alone just makes the chance of staying stuck, stepping back, or holding steady all the more likely. The minute you notice your feelings of fear, stop and identify someone who might be able to support you, and ask for help.

2. *Facts.* Sometimes when we're afraid to move forward, it's because we're missing something—information, a point of view, or the right words to communicate how we feel. For example, let's imagine that you're focused on building your business and you're afraid of selling your products or services. When you ask yourself what's missing, you discover that your inability to act is based on a fear of rejection that's much larger than your desire for success. Needing more information about handling rejection, you may research books, talk to experienced sales people, or even attend a sales seminar. Once you get this information, you'll find that your fear starts to shrink. But it won't necessarily go away completely, which is why you'll need the next step. . . .

3. *Faith.* Once you have the support in place and you've discovered and provided what's missing, the last step has to do with the Almighty leap. Yup, it's like stepping up to the edge of a cold pool, holding your nose, and jumping in. Taking action in spite of your fear helps you to develop faith in the Divine and in yourself. That's the key. Learning to trust that you can handle anything that happens is much more important than whether or not you succeed. And faith only grows when we take action *without*

knowing the end result. So, from now on, when you need to do something scary and you start to waffle—find a friend, get the facts, and seek the faith!

TAKE ACTION CHALLENGE

This week take an inventory of the things you've been avoiding out of fear and pick one item. Next, go through the steps above and challenge yourself to get the support you need so you can take action once and for all.

Remember: even small steps to overcome your fear can make a big difference. For example, if you need to give a speech and you have a fear of public speaking (one of the most common fears of all), you might prepare by teaching a Sunday-school class or reading a good book (Lee Glickstein's *Be Heard Now* is one of the best I've read on this topic).

The one thing I've been afraid to do is:

_____

The friends who can support me are:

_____

The facts I need to research are:

_____

The action I will take this week is:

_____

RESOURCES

Starting from No — Ten Strategies to Overcome Your Fear of Rejection and Succeed in Business by Azriela Jaffe and Pam Lontos (Chicago, Illinois: Dearborn, 1999)

One of the best books I've read on overcoming rejection.

www.womanlinks.com

A wonderful group of women supporting women — discussion list, resources, and help.

Be Heard Now by Lee Glickstein (New York: Broadway Books, 1999)

An excellent, heart-centered guide to overcoming the fear of public speaking.

I Know Just What You Mean: The Power of Friendship in Women's Lives by Ellen Goodman and Patricia O'Brien (New York: Simon & Schuster, 2000)

This book provides an intimate look at the power of friendships.

Week 23

SHINE THE LIGHT

*You are never given a wish without also being given the
power to make it true.*

RICHARD BACH

This week's topic is inspired by the response I received to a four-day retreat idea that I shared with my on-line community. For months I had secretly harbored a desire to share my work in a more intimate setting with a group of people who were interested in stepping off the fast track to consciously create the next year of their lives. To do all this in a beautiful natural setting, while getting massages and enjoying great food, felt like an amazing act of extreme self-care and, I guess, felt too good to be true.

Because this desire was important to me, I held on tight and never let it see the light of day. Sure, I told a few friends and colleagues and even designed the program, but I always stopped short of taking any further action. Truth be told, I didn't want to be disappointed if the project didn't fly. Well, that all changed when a special friend gave me a good stiff nudge and challenged me to put my idea out into the world "just for the fun of it" to see what might happen. Thank God for good friends. Imagine my surprise when my e-mail box quickly filled with excited readers writing, "Yes, tell me more!" What an important lesson!

How often have you kept your most treasured desires a secret—you know, that one thing you fantasize about that no one else knows? The kind of desire that seems too good to be true? Is there something you long to do, be, or offer, that keeps getting put on the back burner? Maybe you'd like to act in a local theater, start a new business, learn to dance, travel for work, or write a book. What stops *you* from making the fantasy a reality?

Sometimes the things we most want seem to come with the most risk — the risk of rejection, disappointment, or failure. But if you play it safe, and never let your desire see the light of day, you risk something even greater — the opportunity to experience the joy that comes from expressing your unique talents and gifts. And worse, by not taking the risk, you're left with a haunting inner voice that will forever sing the song of "if only." What a waste!

What if you were to decide right now to throw caution to the wind and shine a light on your desire? Pull it up to the front burner, make it a priority and share it with the world? What's the worst that could happen?

When the fear comes forward (and it probably will), just remind yourself that no one ever died from disappointment, rejection, or failure — they just got smarter about how to succeed. Go for it!

TAKE ACTION CHALLENGE

This week do something to shine a light on your secret desire. Share your desire with a trusted friend or colleague and ask for their feedback and support (be sure to tell them that you only want *positive* feedback). Take one action to move this dream forward. Sign up for a class, find a mentor, or do something to bring your gifts to the world. You might be pleasantly surprised as things seem to fall into place once you bring your desire to life.

My secret desire is:

_____

To bring it out into the open I will:

_____

One action step I can take this week is:

_____

RESOURCES

Your Heart's Desire by Sonia Choquette, Patrick Tully, and Julia Cameron (New York: Crown, 1997)

An inspiring guide for getting what you want by using your creative abilities.

The Seat of the Soul by Gary Zukav (New York: Simon & Schuster/Fireside, 1999)

This book teaches you to get in touch with your authentic power by aligning your personality with your soul.

Connecting to Creativity by Elizabeth W. Bergmann and Elizabeth O. Colton (Sterling, Virginia: Capital Books, 1999)

A wonderful little book that offers ten keys to unlocking your creative potential.

Wishcraft: How to Get What You Really Want by Barbara Sher (New York: Ballantine Books, 1986)

Still one of the best books around for accomplishing your goals.

Week 24

CLOSE ENCOUNTERS

I have no patience for the cocktail level of life.

NANNA AIDA SVENDSEN

I once had the pleasure of teaching at a beautiful estate nestled on the banks of Long Island Sound. One of the workshops I led was called Building a Soulful Community. During this workshop I was touched by the authenticity of the group that gathered. As we talked about our desire for community, each person acknowledged a deep longing to connect with like-minded people in a soulful, more meaningful way.

It seems that many people feel lonely and isolated in today's busy, electronic age. The need to connect is shared by many. Every client I've worked with and just about every audience member agrees that they'd like more "high-quality" relationships in their lives. It makes sense that this desire would be so strong. Over the last several decades technology and chaotic schedules have driven a wedge between us. Yes, I know that we're told that e-mail and the Internet are actually connecting us, but I don't hear people saying things like, "I wish I'd get more e-mails from the people I care about." Instead, I hear people say that they'd like to spend more time with those they love. They'd like greater intimacy and a chance to share more of their authentic selves.

Fulfilling our need for a deeper connection with others can be challenging. Where do we find these like-minded souls? How do we take an existing relationship deeper? How can we overcome the normal fear of rejection or loss?

The place to start is by remembering that every encounter with another human being is a spiritual encounter, whether we know that person or not. When we stay awake to this truth, it becomes easier to reach out instinctively and open our hearts. We make eye contact for longer. We smile at strangers and say hello. We ask deeper questions of those we care about, taking the conversation to a more intimate level. And when our hearts are open, we're more approachable.

If you'd like to experience more soulful connections in your life, then strengthen your ability to connect. Be present for others. Slow down and make the time to get together. Stop what you're doing when a friend calls and pay attention. Take time out of your busy schedule to spend quality time with your family. When you are with loved ones, take the conversation to a deeper level by asking deeper questions. For example, ask them directly what they've been dreaming about or secretly hoping for in their lives. This will help you move beyond boring, superficial chitchat to a deeper connection.

The possibility for rich relationships exists all around you—you simply have to open your eyes, open your mouth, and most importantly, open your heart.

TAKE ACTION CHALLENGE

This week step out of your comfort zone and risk a deeper connection. If you'd like to take an existing relationship to a new level, tell that person directly. If there's someone you'd like to get to know better, pick up the phone and invite that person to dinner. If you long to bring new relationships into your life, let three people in your community know about it. Remember that since most of us share the same desire, when you reach out, the chances are pretty good that someone will reach back.

The person(s) I'd like to connect more deeply with is (are):

_____

Two people I'd like to get to know better are:

_____

The one action I will take this week is:

_____

RESOURCES

Building a Soulful Community
(audio tape) by Cheryl Richardson
Healing the Whole Self
Conference, November 5–7, 1999
Sounds True
http://www.soundstrue.com
413 S. Arthur Avenue
Louisville, CO 80027
(800) 333–9185

Ed Shea
239 East Wilson
Elmhurst, IL 60126
(630) 530–1060
Coachimago@aol.com

Ed Shea, a relationship coach,
works nationally with couples and
individuals over the phone to help
them enhance communication and
use their relationship as a path
toward personal growth and
healing.

Generations Family Tree Software
by Sierra Home

A fun and thoughtful way to connect with family. All the programs
you need to discover and preserve
your heritage by documenting the
births, deaths, marriages, hard-
ships, and victories that connect
you to your ancestors.

http://www.Ancestry.com

Search over 500 million names in
over 2,000 databases to help you
with your family tree.

ARE YOU A
SPIRITUAL PIONEER?

*There are people who make things happen, those who watch
what happens, and those who wonder what happened.*

UNKNOWN

This past week I had the pleasure of spending five days with special people in a gorgeous part of the country—Boulder, Colorado. While recording an audio program for a company called Sounds True, I had an opportunity to watch what I'd call "spiritual pioneers" in action.

My first encounter came when I arrived at the Coburn House—a beautiful twelve-room inn owned by Sheila and Richard Norris. Sheila and Richard have done an outstanding job of creating a soul-nurturing environment that embraces their guests with the utmost respect and care. From the sign that asks visitors to remove their shoes upon entering their home to the suggestion of reusing towels in order to protect the environment, Richard and Sheila are willing to step out of the box in order to establish a business that honors their personal values.

My next encounter came when I visited Sounds True and spent time with Tami Simon, the president, and her staff. Sounds True is an audio company dedicated to distributing spiritual wisdom to the world. Like Richard and Sheila, Tami and the members of her organization are committed to creating an environment that honors the customer, the community, and each other. At Sounds True, relationships come before results and because of that, the work environment becomes a safe place to which people can bring their inner lives and creative spirits. Both organizations are great examples of how a company can thrive while sticking to the basic spiritual principles of love, truth, and respect for people.

Not all pioneers are spiritual pioneers. Some are dedicated to blazing new trails at the expense of personal values, people, and the environment. But the bar is rising. More and more business owners are realizing that *how* you do business is just as important as bottom-line results. And if the success of the Coburn House and Sounds True are any indication, doing business with honor and integrity makes good fiscal sense, both businesses are thriving by attracting customers that share their values.

We all have the opportunity to be spiritual pioneers in some way. When you put relationships before results, live with integrity, and care about how your actions affect the greater community, you too add spiritual value to the world. Being a spiritual pioneer isn't easy. You may need to be willing to take a stand for what you believe in while others question your sanity. And you might have to turn down a job or a client that challenges you to check your values at the door. But it's the willingness to do things differently that sets you apart from the rest.

To become a spiritual pioneer, you'll need courage and a strength of character that will allow you to step off the common path and stand up to ridicule, criticism, and the inevitable fear, insecurity, and self-questioning that will occur. You'll need to be more interested in honoring your integrity and the greater good than in being well liked. And you'll have to be willing to tell the truth to yourself and others, setting your ego aside for the higher goal of becoming an authentic leader—the kind of leader who makes her own growth a top priority and who ultimately walks his talk.

I don't know about you, but as I raise the bar in my own life, I'm more interested in supporting businesses that are run by spiritual pioneers.

TAKE ACTION CHALLENGE

Become more of a spiritual pioneer in your life by doing one of the following this week:

1. Take a stand for something you believe in, even if others around you think you're crazy.

2. Risk telling the truth even when you're afraid to do so.

3. Honor your Self by referring out any client or customer who is not aligned with your values.

RESOURCES

Sounds True
413 S. Arthur Avenue
Louisville, CO 80027
http://www.soundstrue.com
(800) 333–9185

If you'd like to indulge in a little spiritual wisdom, you can order a catalog by visiting this Web site or giving the company a call.

Coburn Hotel, Sheila and Richard Norris, Owners-Proprietors, Boulder, Colorado
http://www.ra.nilenet.com/~coburn/index.html
Direct Line: (303) 545–5200
Reservations: (800) 858–5811
e-mail: *coburn@nilenet.com*

If you're lucky enough to visit Boulder (and you're willing to take off your shoes), then there's no better place to rest your soul than at the Coburn Hotel.

The Rhythm of Compassion by Gail Straub (Charles E. Tuttle Co., 2000)

A gifted author and teacher, Gail Straub shows readers how they can serve the spirit and the planet simultaneously.

THROW CAUTION
TO THE WIND

Life is short; live it up.

KHRUSHCHEV

While enjoying a bike ride one weekend, I was reminded of how different the world looks from the seat of a bicycle. Unlike the quiet and quickness you experience in a car, spending an afternoon on a bike is like indulging in a sensory feast. Not only was I able to leisurely take in the wonderful sights and sounds of spring—wisteria-framed doorways, lilacs in full bloom, and the laughing seagulls flying overhead—I was also able to revel in the sensuous smells of honeysuckle, sea rose, and backyard barbecues!

As I pedaled through my neighborhood, I smiled to myself as I recalled how I had labored over the decision to buy a bike for more than a year. The truth is that my indecision stemmed from self-consciousness and a fear of the unknown. What if I bought the wrong kind of bike and regretted my purchase? Could I still remember how to ride a bike considering there were now eighteen speeds instead of three? Did I have the physical stamina to actually get somewhere? My fear of not knowing, feeling foolish, or looking silly kept me from enjoying what has become one of my favorite summer pastimes.

Looking back, the decision to buy a bike seems like a silly

thing to feel self-conscious about, and yet it's symbolic of the kind of fear and self-doubt that can keep us from enjoying the simple pleasures of life. Too often we hold ourselves back from the things we'd really like to try, out of a fear of looking foolish, feeling stupid, or making a mistake.

How often have *you* held yourself back from trying something new? What if you could wake up one morning and take a pill that would completely remove your self-consciousness? One little gulp, and your fear of being judged, embarrassed, or looking foolish would completely disappear. What chances would you take? What new things would you try? What fun would you allow yourself?

Our time on this planet is so precious. Why spend so much energy holding yourself back? Let your guard down, throw caution to the winds, and live a little. Once you confront your self-consciousness directly, you'll be surprised at how quickly you get over it. Believe me, when I set out on my first bike ride wearing my "fashionable" new helmet, I got over my fear of looking foolish pretty quickly.

TAKE ACTION CHALLENGE

Is there something you've wanted to do that you've felt self-conscious about? If you're not sure, during the week notice when your self-consciousness prevents you from doing something you'd really like to do. Whether it's smiling at a stranger, asking someone out, learning to roller blade, or making a purchase, challenge yourself to embrace your self-consciousness and do it anyway!

The one thing I've wanted to try is:

_____

The action I will take this week to make it happen is:

_____

RESOURCES

Feel the Fear and Do It Anyway by
Susan Jeffers (New York: Fawcett
Books, February 1992)

This book offers positive thinking
to overcome a variety of common
fears.

The Permission Slip Book
Special Messages 4U
(603) 659–2079
www.specialmessages4u.com

The Original Permission Slip
Book contains 500 individual slips
that tell you what you have done is
okay! Each slip is set with perfora-
tions, so that it's like a coupon that
can be removed from the book.
Post them in an appropriate area
where you or any other recipient
can see them.

Week 27

STANDING IN
THE SHADOW

*One can never consent to creep when one feels
an impulse to soar.*

HELEN KELLER

One of the most common desires we have as human beings is to know and express our purpose in the world—the unique gift or contribution we've come here to share. Frequently I'm asked by audience members to share my thoughts on how we might become more aware of our purpose. My response is usually the following: Shape up the life you already have, and by doing so, your unique contribution will usually reveal itself.

In other words, clean up your environment, creating order and getting rid of anything you no longer need. Assess your relationships, investing more deeply in the connection with loved ones and transforming or ending relationships that drain your energy. Get your financial house in order, so that you're building reserves that will support you. And start saying no to those things that prevent you from honoring your physical, emotional, and spiritual well-being. These are all-important steps that will help to remove the blocks that prevent you from seeing what you've come here to do.

As you're involved in the activities that improve the quality of your life, there is something else you can do to help uncover your unique contribution: notice when you might be standing in the shadow of those people who may be doing what you'd like to do. Let me explain what I mean.

When I was in my mid-twenties, I volunteered (and then worked for) a nonprofit organization in Massachusetts called Interface Foundation. Interface was a holistic education center that hosted authors and speakers like Deepak Chopra, Marianne Williamson, and Carolyn Myss. In my duties as a volunteer, employee, and eventual board member, I often helped with programming ideas, event coordination, and logistics like picking up presenters from the airport. Looking back, I can see that, without realizing it, I put myself in the shadow of those whom I admired or those who were doing what my soul longed to do. I learned quite a bit about what to do and what not to do from standing in the shadows. It's shaped who I am today.

The soul is very wise. Often it will put you with people, or in situations that represent what you've come here to do. For example, you might be working for someone who does what you'd like to do. Or you may be representing the creative efforts of those who are expressing themselves in a way you'd like to express yourself. Maybe you have friends who are in a field that you long to be in? Assessing the friends, businesses, volunteer organizations, or jobs that have frequented your life may hold clues as to what your soul desires.

There is nothing wrong with standing in someone's shadow. It can be a great way to learn. But, if you continue to stand in the shadow of someone who's pretty tall, it might be hard to imagine yourself in his or her shoes. You may need to step out of the shadow and into the light so that you can take your rightful place in the world. So I invite you to pay attention to the shadows you may be hiding in. Is it time for *you* to step into the light?

TAKE ACTION CHALLENGE

During this week take some quiet time and use your journal to review your past and present circumstances, looking for the clues your soul may have created in your life. Notice the kinds of people you've surrounded yourself with. Whom have you admired? What kind of work have you been attracted to? To help identify the experiences that you'd like to explore, take note of those you've supported in the past or the kinds of clients you work with now.

I have been standing in the shadow of:

_____

The people I admire are:

_____

I admire them because:

_____

I have been attracted to the following kinds of work:

_____

The one action I'll take to step out of the shadow is:

_____

RESOURCES

Callings: Finding and Following an Authentic Life by Gregg Michael Levoy (New York: Three Rivers Press, 1998)

Levoy describes the myriad ways to follow your authentic, true work and provides inspiring spiritual and practical guidance.

The Alchemist by Paulo Coelho (New York: HarperPerennial, 1998)

A wonderful fictional tale about the importance of listening to our hearts and finding our own Personal Legend.

Building Your Field of Dreams by Mary Manin Morrissey (New York: Bantam Books, July 1997)

Mary shares her compelling personal story and a practical and inspiring guide for anyone who has ever hoped for a better life.

HOW'S YOUR BACKBONE?

*Work joyfully and peacefully, knowing that right thoughts
and right efforts will inevitably bring about right results.*

JAMES ALLEN

What's the key to living an authentic life that honors your most important priorities? Living with integrity. Integrity is the foundation on which we build our best life. Integrity is our spiritual backbone. When it is straight and strong, life happens more easily. We step into the flow, stay connected to our inner wisdom (our Wise Self), and become a powerful vehicle for divine inspiration. As we pay attention, we begin to get clear messages about what to do next.

Living with integrity means honoring the standards (the internal rules of behavior), that we've set for ourselves. For example, if you have a standard that says, "I always tell the truth," then you'll need to be honest with a friend who has invited you out to dinner when you decide you don't want to go. Instead of making up an excuse, you'll need to tell the truth. Or if you have a standard that says, "I never take something that is not rightfully mine," you'll need to return the extra change you receive from a store clerk when that person has made a mistake.

Living with integrity creates a strong spiritual backbone. When we neglect to honor our standards by going against the rules we've set for ourselves, our spiritual backbone becomes crooked or bent. When this happens, we have a hard time gaining insight, and as a result, life starts to break down. Plans might fall through. We may attract people who drive us crazy. Or doors seem to keep closing regardless of how hard we work. These events can become signals from the universe that our spiritual backbone—our integrity—may be out of alignment.

Because we are unique individuals, we each have different standards by which we live. No one standard is better than another. The important thing is to know *your* standards for living and to honor them so that you can create more divine flow in your life.

The way to live with integrity is to notice where you are not honoring your standards and do something about it. For example, if you are working for an organization that suddenly requires you to work nights and weekends, and you have a standard that says you always have dinner with your family, you may need to make a different arrangement with your boss or look for another job. When you begin to align your actions with the rules you have set for yourself, it's as if you give yourself a "spiritual adjustment" that removes the kinks and bends that can prevent easy access to divine wisdom.

Let's look at some additional examples of living with integrity:

- If you have decided that you will only work with clients who make you happy, then you'll need to turn down the client who drives you crazy, even when that client is offering to pay twice your fee.

- If you've decided that you will not engage in gossip about others, then you'll need to tell your neighbor to stop when he begins talking about the mother down the street.

- When you've decided to be honest in your interactions with others regardless of how difficult it might be, then you'll need to confront a problem with your sister directly rather than avoid the issue or neglect to return her phone calls.

- If, as a leader, you've decided to take responsibility for what your employees do at work, then you may need to step in and resolve a problem immediately without blaming others.

The key to stepping into the flow and creating an authentic life is to be sure that you are living with integrity. So become your own spiritual chiropractor and start adjusting now!

TAKE ACTION CHALLENGE

To determine how well you're living with integrity, answer the following questions:

1. What internal rules have I set for myself?

2. How am I honoring these standards in my everyday life?

3. Where am I not being true to these standards?

Once you have the answers, take action to do something about it.

I need to make an adjustment in the following three situations:

1. _____

2. _____

3. _____

RESOURCES

Coach University's Public Personal Foundation Program
P.O. Box 881595
Steamboat Springs, CO 80488
(800) 48–COACH
www.coachu.com/pfoundation.htm

The Personal Foundation Program is presented in teleclass format for those who want to learn how to easily handle the fundamentals of living.

Divine Intuition: Your Guide to a Life You Love by Lynn A. Robinson (New York: DK Publishing, 2000)

Divine Intuition explores simple ways to help you receive divine guidance through the powerful resource of your intuition.

Radical Honesty: How to Transform Your Life by Telling the Truth by Brad Blanton, Ph.D. (New York: Dell Books, 1996)

An interesting book on truth-telling.

The Children's Book of Virtues by William J. Bennett (New York: Simon & Schuster, 1995)

An enduring compilation of timeless stories designed to lead children toward what is noble, gentle, and fine.

The Adults Book of Virtues by William J. Bennett (New York: Simon & Schuster, 1993)

Time-honored tales to reinforce the essentials of good character: courage, perseverance, responsibility, work, self-discipline, compassion, faith, honesty, loyalty, and friendship.

Your Life Is Your Message by Eknath Easwaran (New York: Hyperion, 1997)

Provides simple lessons about how everything you do influences those around you and how every one of your thoughts and actions influences your own life.

LET FINANCIAL
FREEDOM REIGN

*The main reason people struggle financially is because they
have spent years in school but learned nothing about money.
The result is that people learn to work for money . . . but
never learn to have money work for them.*

ROBERT KIYOSAKI

In *Take Time for Your Life* I wrote about the importance of taking responsibility for the state of your financial health. After working with clients on money issues for more than fifteen years, I've seen a clear link between how well we handle the money we already have and our ability to make more. For example, it was not uncommon for clients who paid their bills late or continued to accumulate debt when they were unable to pay off the debt they already had, to stay stuck in a financial rut. When we're not handling our money in a mature, responsible way, we consistently send a message to ourselves that we're not good stewards for more.

The first step toward financial freedom is to handle the basics. This might mean balancing your checkbook (or paying someone else to do it), eliminating debt, or saving money on a regular basis. When we confront our fear or anxiety about money and take action to improve our financial health, we open the doors for more abundance to come into our lives.

Once you've covered the basics and gotten on the path of financial improvement, the next thing to consider is how well your money is working for you. This chapter is about taking the concept of financial responsibility and building financial reserves to a whole new level.

I'd like to challenge you to invest more seriously (and wisely) in your financial freedom in an even more intentional way. For example, take greater advantage of the power of compound interest. When you finally experience the benefits of earning money on your money and then earning more, and shift your attitude from "working to make money" to "money working for you," the idea of investing takes on a whole new meaning.

Many people have written to tell me about Robert Kiyosaki's book, *Rich Dad, Poor Dad* — a wonderful story with an important message. Having sold more than a million copies worldwide, Kiyosaki has clearly touched a chord with mainstream audiences who are sick and tired of feeling victims to the almighty buck. Kiyosaki (a self-made millionaire) writes about what rich people have known all along: when you focus on educating yourself about money, accumulating assets that work for you, and utilizing the power of compound interest, you invest in your freedom to live life the way *you* want to live it.

So, in the spirit of shifting from "I have a good job that pays me well" to "I'll do what's necessary to create financial independence," I'd like to offer three specific steps to consider.

1. *Get educated about money and investing.* I know most of you are busy and that the thought of delving into investment strategies or stocks and bonds might feel overwhelming, but it doesn't have to be complicated. If money (or a lack of money) controls your life in any way, then why wouldn't you spend some of your time and energy focused on this one important topic? Learning about how to use money to your advantage allows you to take back your power.

For example, you might start by reading *Rich Dad, Poor Dad* (a quick read) so that you have a good solid understanding of the difference between working hard to make money and having money work hard for you. This will give you a strong foundation on which to build your financial freedom. Don't let fear, anxiety, outdated beliefs, or laziness prevent you from getting educated about the one thing that has such a powerful impact on the quality of your life. After all, a lack of financial reserves is the most common excuse I hear for why people are unable to make the kind of choices they want to make in their lives. Rather than staying stuck in a job you hate or an apartment or home that no longer suits you, or feeling trapped by mounting debt, decide to learn as much as you can about how to use money to your advantage.

To make learning fun and easy, pick a newspaper like the *Wall Street Journal* and read it on the way to work, looking for new trends or great investment ideas. Or find a friend who's also interested in taking his or her financial health more seriously and read one book a month (or listen to an audio program) and share what you've learned with each other. Surf the Web. Fool.com has created an amazing resource that allows visitors to learn about a myriad of topics related to money. You can learn about how to use brokerage services, get out of debt, retire rich, conduct stock research, or invest for your kids. You can even open a fictitious account and practice trading stocks on line. Immersing yourself in knowledge about finances will send an even stronger message to yourself that you're paying attention and are able to handle more.

2. *Raise your financial standards and start saving now.* Regardless of how much money you presently have, start shifting your focus from lack to wealth. Recognize that you have the power and ability right now to take control of your financial future. Instead of feeling like a hopeless slave to money, or a job or business you hate, do something about it.

Inside each of us lives a wise financial steward just waiting to come alive. Whether you have lots of debt, are just getting by, or have money that's been sitting in a bank, take your focus off lack or fear and reclaim control over your life by creating smart investments so you can have them working for you.

Save change in a jar and put that money into a bank account each week until you have accumulated enough to go into a mutual fund. Or move your current investments to a more suitable (and lucrative) place. Make sure your money is working for you. The best motivating force for saving money is knowing that you are earning the greatest amount of interest that you possibly can for your personal financial situation. When you're making good money on your money, you're more likely to want to contribute more.

3. *Partner with a financial adviser.* After driving myself nuts for the last year about needing to meet with a financial adviser, I finally set up a meeting. I decided to meet with a "fee only" financial planner, so that I would get independent advice unrelated to any commissions that the adviser might make. The planner was not only a financial adviser but a tax attorney as well. It was the smartest thing I've done to date. Although I have a financial background, spending time with a highly qualified and experienced adviser (someone with an excellent personality, who treated me like a partner) left me feeling excited and inspired to invest more time in my financial health.

Finding the right adviser and making the commitment to review your financial situation from a more holistic perspective will show you the possibilities for your personal financial situation. For example, are you using the power of compound interest to earn you more money? Are you saving money in an investment vehicle that's giving you the best possible return? Are you doing everything you can to reduce your tax liability? These are the kind of questions a good financial adviser can answer and more. Once you learn more and feel as though you have someone on your side, you too will be inspired to raise your financial standards to a whole new level.

Taking better care of your money and investing in your future is about raising your maturity level and facing the reality that a well-paying job may get you only a mediocre life years from now. The belief that a solid education and a good job or successful business are the key to long-term financial success is outdated and not necessarily true. As our economy grows and inflation increases, you may find yourself being forced to endure poor work conditions or an unfulfilling job for a greater part of your life than ever before. And, if you're a business owner whose income depends on your personal labor, you're in the same boat. Be smart. Learn to make your money work for you while you're sleeping, relaxing, or enjoying a vacation!

TAKE ACTION CHALLENGE

This week consider your next steps in moving toward financial freedom. Where are you on the path to financial freedom? Do you need to start saving money? Switch investments you already have? Find a partner to support your efforts? As you think about how you'll make your money work for you, stop and identify one step that you can take this week. For example, you might:

1. Make an appointment with a financial adviser.

2. Visit your local library and pick up a tape program by a financial wizard.

3. Shift your money from the bank to a more lucrative investment account.

4. Invest in your company's 401(k) plan.

5. Cut back on your spending in one area and invest that money.

The one thing I'll do this week to become more educated about money is:

_____

The one action I will take this week to invest in my financial freedom is:

_____

RESOURCES

The Seven Stages of Money Maturity: Understanding the Spirit and Value of Money in Your Life by George Kinder (New York: Dell Books, 2000)

This book not only provides information on saving and investing, it becomes a spiritual guide for understanding and overcoming your emotional blocks about money as well.

Motley Fool Web Site
www.FOOL.com

A great site with a huge selection of information and resources about money and investing.

Debt Counselors of America (DCA)
(800) 680–3328
www.dca.org

This nonprofit organization has so much to offer, from online publications to recommendations for finance software. Visit the Web site or call them twenty-four hours a day.

The Neatest Little Guide to Stock Market Investing by Jason Kelly (New York: Dutton, 1998)

A simple, user-friendly book that tells you everything you need to know about stock-market investing.

Rich Dad, Poor Dad by Robert T. Kiyosaki (Techpress, Inc., March 1999)

A book that tells you what the rich teach their kids about money that the poor and middle class don't.

National Association of Personal Financial Advisors
www.napfa.org
355 West Dundee Road, Suite 200
Buffalo Grove, IL 60089
1–888–FEE–ONLY
info@napfa.org

Dynamic Laws of Prosperity by Catherine Ponder (Devorsse & Co., 1988)

An excellent book on the wisdom of prosperous thinking.

STOP/REFLECT/REWARD

One never notices what has been done; one can only see what remains to be done.

MARIE CURIE

As we move beyond the midpoint of this book, it's a great time to *stop, reflect* on how your life is changing, and *reward* yourself for your accomplishments. It's so common for us to quickly move from one project, goal, or task to the next without stopping to acknowledge what we've accomplished already. We all need acknowledgment and reward, and the very best person to fulfill this need is you!

So, as you review your actions during the first half of this book, take some time to consider the following questions:

1. What changes (small or large) have I made in my life so far?

2. How have I grown as a result of these changes?

3. What have I accomplished?

4. What am I most proud of?

5. In what ways have I been able to make my self-care a priority?

6. How has my relationship with myself improved?

Please give yourself this gift of self-reflection. Using your journal, settle into your favorite soul-nurturing spot, light a candle, and take time to answer each question fully.

Making this exercise a regular practice helps to strengthen your relationship with yourself and sends a very powerful message to your Wise Self that you value and appreciate your commitment to improving the quality of your life. So, this week celebrate your success!

TAKE ACTION CHALLENGE

Once you've spent time answering the questions above, you're ready for the next step. Give yourself a reward for the changes you've made in your life so far. Whether you buy yourself a gift, write yourself a congratulatory letter, or even throw yourself a dinner party—it's important that you *do something* to acknowledge and appreciate your commitment to your self-care.

The five most valuable changes I've made in the last six months are:

1. _____

2. _____

3. _____

4. _____

5. _____

I will reward myself in the following way:

_____

RESOURCES

Proflowers, Inc.
5005 Wateridge Vista Drive
Second Floor
San Diego, CA 92121
(800) 776–3569
www.proflowers.com

Why not send yourself some fresh flowers?

Calyx and Corolla
185 Berry Street, Suite 6200
San Francisco, CA 94107
(888) 88–CALYX

This is another source for the best of the best flowers.

KIDDING AROUND

Too much of a good thing is wonderful.

MAE WEST

One night recently the weather was extremely hot and humid, and later in the evening we were visited by some pesky thunderstorms. After the storms I ventured outside to see if the humidity had broken. As I stepped out the door to take a peek, the feeling in the air instantly reminded of a time in my childhood when, after a rain shower, several of us from the neighborhood ran outside to stomp in warm puddles and get soaking wet.

On a whim I ran upstairs and asked my husband if he'd join me for a late-night walk so I could once again enjoy a few warm puddles. Now this is not typical behavior for me, I'm usually pretty serious. But thank God my husband Michael isn't. Without skipping a beat, he jumped up and said, "Okay!" and we set out for our adventure.

As I stomped through the puddles, I thought about how much I needed more of those childlike moments to balance my serious nature. The kind of carefree, timeless moments that children experience while having only one goal in mind—FUN! How quickly we lose the simple pleasures of childhood. . . .

Walking through the puddles, I realized how important childlike activities are to a busy adult life. So I'd say it's about time we have another fun week, don't you think? (No moaning allowed!) In the spirit of lightening up, here are some suggestions that might help you to reawaken that little kid in you:

- Buy yourself a giant pad of paper and some pastels and schedule a time to draw, using your fingers to smudge the colors together.

- Invite friends over for a meal and forget the silverware. Have your guests eat with their hands (serve spaghetti to really make it fun).

- Buy several cans of Play-Doh and keep them in your office. Create a new monster every week.

- Spend an hour in the woods noticing the height of the trees, the color of the grass, and the little pinecones, sticks and rocks that make for forest jewels.

- Close the shades, put on your favorite dance music, and dance in your living room.

- Get dirty. Go out and weed the yard, plant a tree, or simply dig holes in the dirt.

- Visit a local toy store and spend some time picking out a favorite coloring book (feel free to wear dark glasses and an overcoat if you must). Keep this book in your office and between your adult duties steal some time each day to color.

- Spend an hour sitting on the grass looking for a four-leaf clover.

- Buy a hula hoop and see if you can still swing.

- Have a serious conversation with your dog.

- Get a temporary tattoo.

- Gather together a group of friends for dinner and play musical chairs.

- Get your face painted at a local fair or carnival.

- Grab a friend, buy a watermelon, and have a contest to see how far you can spit the seeds.

- Buy yourself a teddy bear and/or sleep with a stuffed animal.

- Paint your partner's toenails.

- Spend fifteen minutes mimicking your cat.

These are the kinds of things we need to do more often, for no other reason than to upset the apple cart of life and interfere with the rigidity of our daily lives. Trust me, when I returned home from stomping in puddles, with black-bottomed feet, I felt like a million bucks!

TAKE ACTION CHALLENGE

For some of you, engaging in an activity from the above list may seem silly or a bit uncomfortable. If this is the case, then I am especially talking to *you!* Pick one action and do it anyway. You might be pleasantly surprised at how much joy and creativity that little kid of yours adds to your life.

RESOURCES

Camp SARK
(415) 546–3742
*www.campsark.com/campsark/
swwgroups.html*

Visit this site to learn how to hold your own Succulent Wild Woman Group or Party—a great way to connect with other succulent souls!

www.murdermysterygames.com
This Web site has a variety of games for all ages.

ARE YOU A
SLEEPING BEAUTY?

*Health is the first muse, and sleep is the condition
to produce it.*

RALPH WALDO EMERSON

One of the basics of smart self-care is getting a good night's sleep. Recent studies show that more than 40 percent of Americans are sleep-deprived. When I ask audiences to identify ways in which they could practice extreme self-care, inevitably someone talks about needing more sleep.

A good night's rest is one of the most important ways to replenish your energy and enthusiasm for life. When we're sleep-deprived, life loses its luster and can leave us feeling exhausted. Our body needs good solid sleep *every* night. When we're unable to get the kind of sleep we need, this deprivation accumulates and can begin to create havoc in our daily lives. For example, a lack of sleep may leave you:

- unable to focus during the day

- tired and exhausted all the time

- irritable and short-tempered

- depressed or anxious

- more susceptible to colds, headaches, or allergies

- feeling vulnerable and less confident

These symptoms are only some of the ways in which a lack of good rest can negatively impact your life. Unfortunately, too many people learn to tolerate these symptoms and end up short-changing themselves of a higher-quality life.

Stop for a moment and ask yourself how many hours of sleep a night *you* need to feel fully rested, alert, and energized? In our culture we tend to admire those people who can operate on very little sleep. But before electric lights were invented, most people needed ten hours of sleep a night to be fully rested and ready for the day. Set your own standards, then notice whether or not you're able to get the rest you need. Decide right now to do what's necessary to restore this basic self-care habit. Here are some things to consider:

1. Make your bedroom a sanctuary. Since we spend so much time in the bedroom, be sure it's a comfortable, soul-nurturing place to sleep. Is the lighting low and relaxing? Is the room visually clear? Remove any unread books, work, or magazines from your bedroom. When you wake to the sight of these things, your brain automatically becomes stimulated and quickly shifts from a quiet, relaxed state to a more stimulated, analytical mode. Make sure the windows have good shades to keep out streetlights, early morning light, and the like.

2. Don't settle for anything less than *the* perfect bed. When my husband and I upgraded to a new, top-quality king-sized bed, we were shocked by the impact it had on our sleep. Not only did we sleep more deeply and for longer periods of time, we felt much more energized and ready for day. Be willing to try several mattresses before you

make a decision, and be willing to spend money on the right kind of mattress. If you've not changed your mattress in the last five years, visit a good bedding store and try out the new styles of mattresses that are now available. Consider a larger-size mattress too. If you don't need a new mattress, be sure and turn the one you own around at least once a month.

3. Change your sheets more frequently. Although this might sound like a strange tip, you'd be surprised at how responsive the body is to new, fresh smelling sheets, not to mention how much better you'll feel when you cut down on allergens.

4. Speaking of sheets, how comfortable and soft are your sheets? This is another important area to invest in—you deserve high-quality sheets. Give yourself the gift of silk, jersey, or high-thread cotton sheets. Think comfort, comfort, comfort.

5. Remove the television from your bedroom.

6. Choose the best time to go to bed in order to get *your* full night's sleep, and challenge yourself to stick to that schedule every night for the next week so that you can experience the difference in your quality of life. (Yes, *every* night.)

7. Check out the air quality in your bedroom. If you wake with a stuffy nose, headache, or scratchy throat, you might need to use a good air purifier to filter out bacteria, mold or dust (HEPA filters work best). When my husband and I did this, we noticed a difference within one night.

8. Avoid caffeine several hours before going to bed and avoid eating at least four hours before bedtime.

If, after making some of these changes, you're still unable to improve your sleep, consider a visit to a sleep specialist. As a matter of fact, you can visit the National Sleep Foundation Web site for more information on sleep disorders and to check your sleep IQ by visiting *http://www.asda.org*

Sleep well!

TAKE ACTION CHALLENGE

This week take an inventory of your bedroom and sleep habits, and improve upon one area. You might remove the television from your bedroom, schedule a shopping trip to a mattress store, go to bed earlier, or buy a new set of sheets. Help your body and mind rest, relax, and rejuvenate.

In addition to making the necessary changes that will transform your bedroom into a sleep sanctuary, there is a relaxation exercise I'd like to recommend.

I've found this "balanced breathing" exercise to be very helpful. This technique comes from the book *Instant Emotional Healing* by George J. Pratt and Peter T. Lambrou. It focuses on balancing the body's energy field so that you can feel more deeply relaxed.

When you're ready to sleep, lie on your back and breathe gently . . .

1. Cross your left ankle over your right ankle.

2. Extend both arms straight out in front of you.

3. Cross your right arm over your left arm at the wrist.

4. Rotate the palms of your hands so that they are facing and interlock your fingers.

5. Rotate your hands down toward your stomach.

6. Continue rotating inward so that you bring your hands up close to your chest. At this point you have crossed the center line of your body with your hands, arms, and legs.

7. Once in the proper position, inhale through your nose while touching the tip of your tongue to the roof of your mouth. Exhale through your mouth, resting your tongue on the floor of your mouth.

While breathing, focus your thoughts on the concept of balance. You might visualize a balanced scale or seesaw, or repeat the word "balance" over and over in your mind. Continue with this process for at least two minutes.

In addition to using this relaxation technique, also complete the following:

The areas that need to be improved in my bedroom are:

1. _____

2. _____

3. _____

The one change I'll make this week is:

_____

RESOURCES

Good Nights: How to Stop Sleep Deprivation, Overcome Insomnia, and Get the Sleep You Need by Dr. Gary Zammit (Kansas City: Andrews McMeel Publishing, 1998)

A noted sleep-disorder expert has the answers to overcoming insomnia, ending sleep deprivation, and getting the proper amount of sleep.

The Sleep Solution: A 21-Night Program to Better Sleep by Dr. Nigel Ball and Nick Hough (Berkeley, California: Ulysses Press, 1998)

For the thirty million Americans who suffer from insomnia, this clear, concise handbook of practical information offers help in the form of a twenty-one-day program for restful sleep.

American Sleep Disorders Association (ASDA)
www.asda.org

Professional medical association representing practitioners of sleep medicine and sleep research.

National Sleep Foundation
729 15th Street NW, Fourth Floor
Washington, DC 20005
www.sleepfoundation.org

Founded in 1990, this organization is nonprofit and promotes public understanding of sleep and sleep disorders and supports sleep-related education and research.

SPRING-CLEAN YOUR OFFICE

Analyze your life in terms of its environment. Are the things around you helping you toward success —or are they holding you back?

W. CLEMENT STONE

While visiting a friend at her high-rise office in the city, I was reminded of the days when I worked in a stuffy corporate office with a window that looked out over a building. During that time in my professional life I often suffered from headaches, sinus problems and low energy in the afternoons. As I sat talking to my friend, I could actually feel my body start to lose energy. And when I began yawning at inappropriate times, I knew I needed some fresh air.

Since so many of us spend a good amount of time in an office every day, it's important to make sure that our work environment isn't harmful to our health. Much like a bad mattress that continually robs our body of sleep, the consequences of working in an unhealthy office environment can become more serious over time. Frequent colds and flu, sinus problems, and dramatic shifts in energy are just some of the common complaints that I've heard from clients over the years.

It's easy to forget the impact that your office has on your day-to-day health and effectiveness. An office that's disorganized, poorly lit, or filled with stale air can drain your energy or, worse, make you sick. So, whether you have an office in your home, a cubicle at the company, or a high-rise suite downtown, you might want to consider the following:

1. *How clean is your office?* Along with getting rid of piles and clutter (remember: when in doubt, throw it out!), it's important that your office is cleaned on a regular basis. This might mean eliminating dust and dirt, vacuuming the floors, and washing the windows. If you work for a company that uses a cleaning service, don't be afraid to finish the job if your office is not cleaned thoroughly. Whether you do it yourself or hire someone else to do it, a thorough cleaning is always a good place to start (and it's good feng shui too!).

2. *How is the lighting?* Does the lighting in your office make for a comfortable work atmosphere? Do your eyes get tired easily during the day? Check out the lighting near your desk or the light reflected on your computer screen. Turn off overhead florescent bulbs. Some people are actually allergic to certain kinds of florescent lighting, which can cause their eyes to water or itch. Instead, you might want to use a small, bright desk lamp. And consider using full-spectrum light bulbs to help give your body much needed sunlight (especially if you're indoors most of the day). Changing the lighting will not only make it easier to see while working, it can also enhance the mood and atmosphere of any office (even cubicles!).

3. *How well can you breathe?* Air quality is key to a healthy work environment, and recent studies show that the quality of air we breathe in our home or office may be more damaging than we think. If you're working in a closed, ventilated building without windows (or without a way to open a window), then there's a good chance that you're breathing recycled air. Why not add a small air filter/purifier with a HEPA filter to your office?

4. *How close by is clean water?* By now we all know that our bodies need to stay hydrated during the day, especially if you work in a stuffy office. I increased my intake of water by installing a hot-cold water cooler next to my desk. The investment (less than $25 per month) has allowed me to have clean, fresh water available at arm's length all day long. Water is a must for self-care at work.

5. *Does your office have creature comforts?* Too often we think of an office as "the place to work" and forget that we'll be much happier and productive when we actually enjoy the space. Why not add a little comfort to your home away from home? For example, add some life to your office—literally. Add a flowering plant, indoor tree, or fresh flowers. Add some unusual comforts. I once had a boss who kept a sheepskin foot warmer under his desk. During the winter months he'd step into his office, slip out of his shoes, and place his feet on a warm, cozy spot under his desk. Other creature comforts might include:

- comfortable slippers, shoes or socks

- stereo or walkman for your favorite music

- candles, incense, or an aromatherapy diffuser

- small bubbling water fountain

- your favorite artwork or photographs

- a DO NOT DISTURB sign

- wind chimes for a window

- comfortable pillow for your chair

As you spend time creating a healthier, more enjoyable work environment, think of this as an investment in your professional success. After all, once you've created a healthy, happy office, you'll be healthier. You'll have more energy, be more relaxed, and be in a much better mood. Sounds like good business to me!

TAKE ACTION CHALLENGE

Take some time this week to assess each of the areas mentioned above. Start with one area and begin to implement changes this week. If you're unsure of what to do or feel that you're too busy, ask for help. Hire someone to clean the office or ask a spouse or friend to lend a helping hand.

The three things I'll do to improve my office are:

1. _____

2. _____

3. _____

RESOURCES

Gaiam, Inc.
www.gaiam.com
(303) 464–3600

Provider of information, goods, and services to customers who value the environment, a sustainable economy, and healthy lifestyles. You can contact Gaiam, Inc. to request their catalogs—*Harmony* and *Innerbalance*—to find products that will help you create a healthier environment.

The Austin Healthmate Air Purifier
Phillips Publishing, Inc.
7811 Montrose Road
P.O. Box 59750
Potomac, MD 20859–9750
(800) 705–5559

Stephanie Winston's Best Organizing Tips: Quick, Simple Ways to Get Organized and Get on with Your Life by Stephanie Winston (New York: Simon & Schuster/Fireside, 1996).

Stephanie Winston gives you all the best tips to help you simplify your daily life.

500 Terrific Ideas for Organizing Everything by Sheree Bykofsky (New York: Budget Book Service, 1997)

This book offers no-nonsense solutions for organizing schedules, creating filing systems, rearranging closets, managing ideas, and other projects.

www.furniturefind.com
(800) 362–SOFA (7632)

Name-brand furniture delivered to your door in the continental United States. Also, coming soon, an online furniture auction for used products.

STRETCH YOURSELF

Feel the fear and do it anyway.

SUSAN JEFFERS

When Joann and Scott decided to open a day-care center for low-income families in their community, they never expected a last-minute crisis. Two days before the closing on the property that would house the center, the bank notified them of an additional $8,000 that they would need to add to their existing down payment. With all their resources in use, Joann and Scott felt stuck. Where would they get the money? And how would they raise the funds so soon?

After getting over the initial shock, Joann and Scott realized that they'd need to reach out to their community and ask for help (even to those community members without children). Asking for money was the last thing they wanted to do, and yet, in order to succeed with their plans, they realized that at this late date they had no other choice.

Asking for and receiving help is more challenging than we might think. It was a real stretch for Joann and Scott to ask for money. Because they would personally benefit from the success of the center, they felt awkward and uncomfortable. Yet they were challenged to reach beyond their fear of what others might think in order to serve their higher vision—that the people in their community have the necessary day care they needed to find work that would support their families. When they asked for help, the community responded.

The fact that Joann and Scott were serving a larger vision with their business made it easier to ask for help. They had learned long ago that it was important to link their personal success to a larger vision. Otherwise, they knew, their achievements would ultimately be empty and meaningless. Success without a larger vision gets old real fast. Instead of feeling fulfilled, you keep wanting more.

When you're working for a greater good, it often becomes easier to stretch yourself and do something that feels uncomfortable. For example, when you care about your son's school policy, you might challenge yourself to speak up at a PTA meeting in spite of the fear you feel. Or, if protecting the environment is important to you, you may reach outside of your comfort zone and take on a recycling project in your community. You no longer let your fear or discomfort, your "smallness," get in your way.

Being afraid of what people might think about you is a good example of the kind of smallness that will prevent you from honoring your higher vision. Once you're clear about your vision — how your contribution and work is linked to a greater good — it can become an anchor that will keep you rooted in what matters most. This will allow you to stretch beyond your smallness.

How is what you're doing in your life right now serving the world? And most important, what do you need to overcome in order to bring your commitment to a whole new level? If you're not sure, see if any of the following might be standing in your way:

- Your fear of the reactions of others

- Your fear of failure

- Your fear of too much responsibility

- Your inability to ask for help

- Your inability to receive help
- Your fear of rejection
- Your fear of being judged or criticized
- Your fear of disappointment

We never do great things alone. Whether your vision is to be the best parent in the world, serve your local community, or help heal the planet in some way, you will never do anything of greatness by yourself. And as long as we need other people, our fears and concerns about others will always hold us back.

Start stretching yourself right now. If you're afraid of what people might think, challenge yourself to do something wild or uncharacteristic and face the consequence head on. If you have a hard time asking for help, ask ten people a day for something — directions, support, information, anything — until you get better at it. If you're so afraid of the additional responsibility that comes with playing bigger in the world (and yes, there is more) then put the support systems in place *now* to handle it so you can keep moving forward.

The good news is that we need not face our fears alone. As a matter of fact, with the love and support of others we can reach beyond our fear and realize our vision much more quickly.

TAKE ACTION CHALLENGE

There are two parts to this week's Take Action Challenge. First develop a clear vision for your work. If you're unsure, spend some time answering the following questions:

How does my work serve others?

How do I want it to serve a greater good?

Write down all the thoughts, feelings, and ideas that come to mind. Next, put the answer into one simple sentence. For example, you might decide that "I contribute to a healthy society by raising my child to be a loving, compassionate adult" or, "I contribute to the protection of the earth by working in our local recycling center." Don't worry about developing the perfect vision; it will evolve over time.

Once you've done this step, identify one fear or concern that might be holding you back from pursuing this vision in a larger way. When you've got one in mind, choose someone you respect from your community to support you in challenging this fear.

My vision is:

_____

The one fear that might prevent me from supporting this vision is:

_____

This week I will ask _____ to help me overcome this fear.

RESOURCES

The Path: Creating Your Mission Statement for Work and for Life by Laurie Beth Jones (New York: Hyperion, 1996)

A great little book that will guide you through the process of identifying and fulfilling your personal mission.

The Invitation by Oriah Mountain Dreamer (New York: HarperCollins, 1999)

The author uses passages from her original Internet poem, "Invitation," to welcome readers into a life that has far greater truth and integrity.

FEATHERING YOUR NEST

Mid pleasures and palaces though we may roam,
Be it ever so humble, there's no place like home.

JOHN HOWARD PAYNE

This chapter is inspired by a shopping trip my husband Michael and I took one weekend to find a rug for our library. For more than two years I had allowed this favorite spot in our home to go unfinished because of my busy writing and speaking schedule. What a mistake. Once we found the perfect rug to fit the spot, I felt inspired. By adding a beautiful antique lamp, my favorite chair, and a log on the fire, I was soon enjoying a new soul-nurturing place in our home. It's amazing how "beauty" can feed the soul!

What about your home? Is there a special place for your soul to sit, relax, and rejuvenate? A spot filled with beauty that makes you smile even when you walk by? I know, I can hear some of you groaning (especially those of you with children) as you think about how challenging it can be sometimes just to find a clear space to walk, let alone enjoy. But it's important to remember that even a little beauty goes a long way. Small changes to a room can make a difference. For example, when I lived alone in a small apartment in the city, I added a small bird feeder to my bedroom window. Each morning I'd wake to the sweet chirps of yellow or red finches having breakfast.

Waking in the morning to a view of trees or birds is far more soul-nurturing than waking to a pile of unread books by your bed. Why not get rid of the books and move your bed by a window? Listening to the gentle bubbling of a water fountain calms the nerves so much better than the constant hum of the traffic passing by. These simple changes can turn an ordinary room into a soul-nurturing haven. Don't underestimate the powerful effect that your environment has on you.

TAKE ACTION CHALLENGE

This week give yourself permission to do something special that will help create a soul-nurturing space in your home. For example, you might add a wind chime to a window or place a sweet-smelling jasmine plant on a table nearby. Why not enjoy the gentle fragrance of incense (Blue Pearl Classic Champa is wonderful) or hang up that favorite picture you've wanted to get framed. Maybe *you* have a rug you've been meaning to buy. Whatever it is, add a feather to your nest and give your soul a warm, comfortable place to rest.

- Choose a special spot in your home.

- Clean it thoroughly.

- Assess the space and determine those things you'd like to add (lighting, accessories, or comfortable furniture).

- Add one thing this week.

RESOURCES

Design Views
http://www.designviews.com
This site contains a wealth of information on interior design including a great online magazine and shopping guide.

Use What You Have Decorating by Lauri Ward (New York: Perigee, September 1999)

Transform your home in one hour with ten simple design principles, using the space you have, the things you like, the budget you choose.

Book of Candles: A Practical and Creative Guide to Using Candles in Your Home by Miranda Innes with Clive Streeter (photographer) (New York: DK Publishing, 1977).

To help warm your environment, here are all types of candles, including beeswax, decorated, Christmas, and floating varieties, plus many types of holders.

BRING IN THE RESERVES

Money cannot buy peace of mind. It cannot heal ruptured relationships, or build meaning into a life that has none.

RICHARD M. DEVOS

If I asked you to consider how *secure* you feel in your life right now, what would you think of first? If you're like most people you probably equate a sense of security with how much money you have. For example, you might think about your investments and wonder whether or not you'll have enough saved to care for yourself and your family when you retire. I know I did. In order to feel secure, I focused on earning and saving money as a way to achieve peace of mind. Unfortunately the feelings of security and peace didn't seem to increase with my bank account alone. Regardless of how much money I earned or saved, I never felt quite secure. I've since learned an important lesson—the key to creating true security has to do with more than the balance in your savings account. It has to do with the balances in other accounts as well.

I'll never forget a conversation I had with my first coach about security. During the call I complained about never feeling secure enough regardless of how much money I earned. After spending a good amount of time investing in my financial health and saving money, I had far more choices than ever before, but I still didn't have the peace of mind I desired. I wanted to know when enough would be enough.

When I finished complaining, he offered me some great advice. He said, "Cheryl, true security comes from having a reserve in *all* areas of your life — community, love, self-esteem, a connection to God, and health, in addition to financial reserves. Until you invest in these other areas, you'll always feel insecure, regardless of how much money you have."

That one sentence changed the way I looked at security forever. I realized that I was stuck in an old way of thinking.

We live in a work-centered culture. This culture encourages us to seek security by working, earning money, saving money, and working some more. The goal of this process is to accumulate enough wealth to retire in comfort. But an *overfocus* on work and earning money creates a problem. As long as you believe that money is the key to security, you'll keep working hard, neglecting to invest in other areas of your life. And without taking the time to invest in your relationships, a spiritual practice, or your emotional and physical health, you'll never experience a sense of security. So you just keep working harder. Get the picture?

Of course money is important; as I mentioned in an earlier chapter, we all need money in order to make the kind of choices that improve the quality of our lives. But it's equally important to make deposits into other accounts as well. For example, ask yourself the following questions:

1. Do I have a reserve of friends and family by whom I feel loved and supported?

2. Do I have a reserve of confidence and self-esteem?

3. Do I have a reserve of faith and a strong connection with God?

4. Do I have a reserve of physical energy?

5. Do I have a reserve of colleagues who challenge and inspire me to be my best?

Just as you make regular deposits into your savings account, you'll want to start making regular deposits into these other accounts as well. When you view security from this perspective, you begin to realize that regular dates with your best friend are just as important as regular deposits into your IRA. And that building a reserve of self-esteem by setting boundaries with someone who drains your energy or taking good care of your needs is even more important than putting money away for a new home.

It takes time and attention to build reserves in each of these areas. The important thing is to raise your level of awareness and realize that when you build reserves in every area of your life, you not only make for a secure future, you create a secure present as well. And living in a secure present means you'll make much better choices that make for a much better life!

TAKE ACTION CHALLENGE

This week schedule some time to assess your various accounts. Take a large sheet of paper and create several columns. At the top of each column list a category such as love, community, confidence/self-esteem, emotional and physical health, and so on.

Once you've completed these columns, write down your current balance in each of these areas. For example, under "community" you might list close friends and family members; under physical health you might list those things that you already do to take good care of your body.

Once you're clear about what you *do* have, pick one area that you'd like to invest more energy in and make a deposit this week!

RESOURCES

Energy of Money by Maria
Nemeth, Ph.D. (New York:
Wellspring, 2000)

A spiritual guide to finance
and personal fulfillment.

Courage to Be Rich by Suze Orman
(New York: Riverhead Books,
March 1999)

This book will help you to create a
life of material *and* spiritual abundance.

FIX WHAT'S BROKEN

The time to repair the roof is when the sun is shining.

JOHN F. KENNEDY

One day, while driving to meet with friends, I hit a traffic jam and picked up my car phone to call and let them know I'd be a bit late. As I dialed the phone, the power kept cutting out, and my frustration grew as I reminded myself for the fifteenth time that I needed to get a new phone.

Little annoyances like this one are the kind of things that can drive you crazy and downshift your mood instantly. Unfortunately we often discover these annoyances in the middle of trying to do something important. For example, you might be rushing off to an important appointment only to discover that you forgot to get gas for the car. Or you've got a big day at work, and when you reach into your closet to pull out your favorite suit, you discover the missing button you've been meaning to fix. And, there's always the filing that's been building up for weeks (or months) that makes it impossible to find that one piece of paper you desperately need during a phone call with a customer.

In the past when I've suggested that clients handle these annoyances *before* they become a bigger problem, I usually hear things like, "I don't have enough time as it is," or "I have more important things to do." Well, I've learned from experience that scheduling time on a regular basis to handle the little annoyances not only prevents enormous frustration later on, it actually saves time and makes you more productive.

As we continue on the Life Makeover path taking steps to improve your life, this week's task is to take care of those things that have been driving you crazy. Is there something that needs to be repaired or replaced around your home or office? Are there supplies that need to be replenished before you run out? Do yourself a favor and schedule some time this week to embark on the Take Action Challenge below. You'll be surprised at how taking the time to handle the little things makes a big difference in the quality of your life. And it prevents small annoyances from becoming bigger problems later on.

TAKE ACTION CHALLENGE

Your challenge this week is to identify and eliminate five little annoyances that have been driving you crazy. Stop right now and consider some of the areas where these pesky tasks might be — your car, your office, your home, or maybe your wardrobe. If you have trouble coming up with examples, keep a piece of paper in your wallet or purse, and each time you stumble upon something that you've been meaning to do, make a note. By the end of the week, I'm sure, you'll have at least five examples to tackle over the weekend. Good luck!

The five things I'll handle this week are:

1. _____

2. _____

3. _____

4. _____

5. _____

PRESEASON CHECKUP

*When you focus on free time, you multiply
your productivity.*

SUSAN CORBETT

The beginning of autumn is the time of the year that always leaves me feeling a bit sad. I enjoy the slower pace of summer so much that the idea of shorter days and cold weather leaves me wishing for just one more month.

Each summer I spend at least two weeks living in the beauty of nature without any scheduled plans, ringing phones, or e-mail messages to pull me away from myself. I sleep as long as I want, write endless pages in my journal, and sit at the beach enjoying the sun. During this "sabbatical for the soul" I always realize how important it is for me to take an extended period of spontaneous time away to let my mind settle. As the days go by, I feel more at peace and naturally begin to shift my focus inward in order to reevaluate my priorities. It's the perfect way to end the summer.

For many of us the end of summer signals a new year, a time to swing into action and get back to the serious business of work. This mentality, I'm sure, stems from our younger years, when the spontaneous days of summer vacation were replaced with schedules, school classes, and too much homework.

Before plunging back into work, you might want to take some time to reevaluate your priorities and tighten your commitment to your self-care—the key to a smooth and joyful transition. You can start by considering the following questions:

- Have you reevaluated your priorities (your Absolute Yes list) so that you are clear about the top five things you most want to give your time and attention?

- Have you scheduled weekly time for yourself over the next three months in ink (especially during the holiday season)?

- Have you made any commitments that now require a change of heart? Remember, changing your mind is always a fair option, and it's better to do it sooner rather than later.

As you consider your upcoming schedule, look for those areas that might cause you to feel overwhelmed and handle them now. For example, if you're a mom with kids who will need to be carpooled all over the place for extracurricular activities, contact several other moms and make arrangements to share the driving. (Believe me, the other moms will be relieved too!)

Don't rush out of summer and into the new season headfirst! Stay connected to your body and your soul by scheduling time for yourself and revisiting your top priorities so that you'll be sure to spend your energy on those things that matter most.

When I returned from our family's annual Labor Day reunion, I smiled to myself as I remembered the faces of my nieces and nephews. The vision of them splashing in the ocean and building sand castles on the beach not only reminds me of what really matters, it's also the memory that tides me over to next summer.

TAKE ACTION CHALLENGE

Set aside an evening or an afternoon this week for a preseason checkup. Use this time to:

1. Update your Absolute Yes list. Make a separate list for personal and professional priorities, put them on 3x5-inch index cards, and keep them in view.

2. Review your calendar for the next three months and cancel any commitment that makes you feel a sense of dread or regret.

3. Create a "reserve of space" by scheduling weekly self-care breaks from now until the first of January.

4. Choose a weekend during the next three months and give yourself the gift of a sabbatical for your soul.

RESOURCES

BED AND BREAKFAST RESOURCE

www.bedsandbreakfastsandinns.com

If you'd like to set up a few weekends away, this Web site lets you book on-line reservations at thousands of places to stay throughout the world.

www.SelfCare.com

This Web site is designed to help you take care of you and your family's health and wellness needs.

www.slowlane.com

A terrific on-line self-care resource for dads and their families.

SETTLE FOR MORE

If you must compromise, compromise up.

ELEANOR ROOSEVELT

I had tea with a good friend who shared a personal story that inspired the topic for this chapter. A traveling sales associate with a large electronics company, Sandy had the following tale to tell:

WHILE TRAVELING for my job, I arrived at the airport for one of my flights, and discovered that the gate attendant who handled my seat assignment had mistakenly booked me in a center seat at the back of the plane—the last place a frequent traveler like myself wants to sit.

I was originally told that the plane was much larger than it was, and when I arrived at my seat, I realized that I needed to make a change. When I turned around to head up front, I was faced with a long line of passengers waiting for me to put my luggage in the overhead compartment so they could get to their seats. I sat down feeling frustrated and annoyed. As the passengers continued to board, I started a conversation in my head that went something like this: "Well, one trip in a bad seat won't kill you, Sandy. The flight seems full, there are too many people trying to board, and you'll only cause problems if you try to change seats now." I even tried the process of "just breathe and use this situation as an opportunity to practice acceptance." Then I snapped out of it.

When the aisle cleared a bit, I left my bag in the overhead bin and quickly moved to the front of the plane. I politely explained the situation to the flight attendant and asked for a better seat. The flight attendant, who was extremely pleasant, asked me to step aside and wait. Several minutes later she returned and led me to the aisle seat in the bulkhead section of the plane (one of my favorite seats). I was so glad that I'd spoken up!

What's the moral of this story? Don't settle for less.

This simple experience is an example of the kind of rules that many of us live by: Don't rock the boat. Be nice. Put the needs of others before your own. Don't make a scene. Settle for less. For example, have you ever asked for a meal to be prepared in a special way at a restaurant, only to be served the wrong dish and eaten it anyway? Or decided against buying a CD player for your new car because it cost a little bit more than you thought you should spend? Maybe you've stayed in a relationship that you've outgrown in order to protect the other person's feelings.

The bottom line is that we always get what we settle for. When you risk rocking the boat, disappointing others, or giving yourself more than you think you deserve, you automatically raise your standards. Now I'm not suggesting that you become a diva or act in such an arrogant way that you appear rude or insensitive. I'm just encouraging you to become more aware of your needs so that you can treat them (and yourself) with the respect and consideration they deserve.

So the next time you find yourself having the same kind of conversation in your head, remember that settling for a bad seat in an airplane or the wrong meal in a restaurant may only be a small example of what you settle for in your life. Start settling for more!

TAKE ACTION CHALLENGE

This week pay attention to where you settle for less in your life. You might even want to make a sign for your office or a note card for your appointment book that says:

"Are you settling for more?"

Use this sign to remind yourself to raise your standards. Whether it's food in a restaurant, the quality of an item that you purchase, or the way you allow yourself to be treated in a relationship, challenge yourself to speak up and ask for what you want.

I settle for less in my life when I:

_____

The three changes I'd like to make are:

1. _____

2. _____

3. _____

RESOURCES

A Woman's Worth by Marianne Williamson (New York: Ballantine Books, 1993)

A wonderful little book for both men and women about understanding and acknowledging your value.

Coach Yourself to Success by Talane Miedaner (Chicago, Illinois: Contemporary, 2000)

This book will show you how to raise your standards and get much more out of life.

PAMPER BREAK

*Are you ready and willing to become a person who actively
responds to the good things in life?*

JUDI HOLLIS

I t's time again for a little self-indulgence. Sad to say, most of us
who lead busy lives need to be reminded of when to give ourselves the gift of self-care. It's time to do your body, mind, and
spirit a big favor. Pick something from the list below or choose
your own special self-care treat, and do something about it *this
week!*

You might:

1. Schedule an hour-and-a-half massage.

2. Get a manicure and a pedicure (men too!).

3. Schedule afternoon tea with a favorite friend.

4. Find a cozy inn and book a romantic evening.

5. Take a warm bath in the middle of the day and read a favorite book.

6. Rent two of your all-time favorite movies, turn the ringer
   off on the phones, and spend an afternoon or evening in
   bed watching them.

7. Take a mental-health day off from work.

8. Do something special with the kids, like getting dressed up for dinner.

If you're reading this chapter and thinking, "I already do lots of great things for myself," then that's wonderful—you're way ahead of the game. Now raise the bar and do something even better!

If you're not sure of what to do, ask yourself the following question:

"What kind of self-care gift have I been daydreaming about or wishing for?"

When you hear the answer, write it down and make it happen!

TAKE ACTION CHALLENGE

Please don't read this chapter, think it's a nice idea, and then put the book down. Pick up the phone or your appointment book and schedule something right now!

RESOURCES

Cinematherapy by Nancy Peske and Beverly West (New York: Dell, 1999)

A great guide for women who like to search for movies that fit their mood.

The Woman's Comfort Book by Jennifer Louden (San Francisco: Harper, 1992)

This book provides a wealth of self-care ideas.

Simple Abundance: A Day Book of Comfort and Joy by Sarah Ban Breathnach (New York: Warner Books, November 1995)

A practical, inspirational daily guide that provides a meditation or exercise for every day of the year to help women pare down their lives and clear their mental clutter.

Associated Bodywork & Massage Professionals (ABMP)
28677 Buffalo Park Rd.
Evergreen, CO 80439-7347
(800) 458–2267
www.abmp.com

Will provide information on the benefits of massage, bodywork, and somatic therapies, as well as help in locating practitioners.

American Polarity Therapy Association (APTA)
2888 Bluff St., Suite 149
Boulder, CO 80301
(303) 545–2080
www.polaritytherapy.org

This organization provides information on the study and practice of Polarity Therapy.

The Essentials of Yoga by Dinabandhu Sarley, Ila Sarley, Omega Institute (New York: Dell Books, 1999)

A great Yoga book from the Omega Institute Mind, Body, Spirit Series.

Yoga Journal for Health & Conscious Living
P.O. Box 469088
Escondido, CA 92046
(800) 600–9642

This magazine is a self-published bimonthly and provides updated timely information on yoga and related subjects. Subscription: $21.95 for 1 year (6 issues).

SELF-CARE AT WORK

The first step toward success is taken when you refuse to be a
captive of the environment in which you first find yourself.

MARK CAINE

Recently I received an e-mail from a reader who, after spending the last three months on sabbatical, had been offered a new position with a terrific company. She and the company recognized that this new job fit her talents, skill level, and values perfectly. The company was very excited about having her join their team, yet she felt nervous about moving forward. She worried about how her life would be affected by the transition from a healthy, more balanced lifestyle to what she assumed would be a fast-paced, demanding schedule. My advice to her was simple: since you call the shots, play by new rules.

Whether you're starting a new job, running your own business, or working for a company already, you have a choice about how you work. You can make your self-care a priority and be more productive and effective, or you can continue to believe that sixty-hour work weeks and a frenetic pace equal greater success.

Although there are many goals that drive an organization, the primary goal of business is to make money. That's just a basic fact. In order to achieve the company objectives and keep people employed, the organization needs to increase its bottom line (profit) on a consistent basis. That's why most companies get worried when employees start talking about work-life balance issues. They make the mistake of believing that supporting self-care strategies at work will promote laziness, selfishness, and unproductive activities. This may be true for some employees, but experience has shown me that the best and the brightest people always end up producing better results.

It is a myth to believe that working long hours at a frantic pace makes you productive. By now most of us recognize that overwork and stress cause everything from a lack of creativity to stress-related illnesses that diminish our effectiveness. Taking better care of yourself makes good business sense. If you don't believe me, try an experiment. Incorporate some of the new rules below for the next thirty days and see what happens. If you adopt some of these rules *and* put them into practice, you'll find that you not only get more done at work, you'll have more time for your life.

NEW RULES FOR TWENTY-FIRST-CENTURY BUSINESS

1. I take lunch every day and do something unrelated to work. For example, I get out of the office and take a walk, listen to a relaxation tape, write in a journal, read a book, or visit with a friend.

2. I work reasonable hours. On most days, I arrive at _____ and leave by _____.

3. I schedule "breathing room" every day so I can step back, reevaluate my priorities and be sure that I am working on what really matters.

4. I do whatever it takes to create a healthy work environment. I keep my office free of clutter, and if necessary, I use a clean air filter and, full spectrum lighting, and I keep a reserve of bottled water nearby.

5. I have an Absolute Yes list for work (a 3x5-inch index card with my top five priorities listed in order of importance), and I refer to it often.

6. I train myself to consistently look for ways to delegate work in order to empower others.

7. I hire only highly competent, talented people to support my efforts.

8. I ask family and friends to honor my work time by eliminating nonessential personal calls and interruptions.

9. I coordinate my work schedule to remove distractions and interruptions. For example, I design blocks of uninterrupted, focused time, and I only check voice mail and e-mail twice a day.

10. I stop taking on more than I can handle. When asked to take on a project, I check to be sure that I can complete the assignment without suffering or sacrificing my self-care.

Think of these rules as part of a twenty-first-century job description. Putting them into practice may be challenging at first, but I can assure you that if you do, you'll be more effective at work and more relaxed at home. To ensure your success, you might ask a coworker, fellow self-employed friend, or partner to try the thirty-day experiment with you.

If you work for someone else, set up a meeting with your boss to discuss how this new idea might benefit you both. Explain that you'd like to try an experiment and ask for your boss's approval. Let your boss (and/or coworkers) know ahead of time that you'll be using these new rules to challenge yourself to be more focused and productive during the day. Invite them to join you in this experiment as you discover how self-care at work translates into bottom-line results.

TAKE ACTION CHALLENGE

Create your own twenty-first-century job profile. Retype the above list and customize it to fit your needs. When you have your new rules in place, print out the list and hang it on the wall in your office. Review the list each day this week and pay close attention to how your workday and personal life improve over time.

RESOURCES

The Heart Aroused by David Whyte (New York: Doubleday Currency, June 1996)

David demonstrates the power of prophecy, poetry, and enlightenment to give voice and strength to our most creative but most hidden desires.

Gathering: A Search for Balance and Fulfillment by Sandra Finley Doran and Dale Finley Slongwhite (Nampa, Idaho: Pacific Press, 1999)

A collection of tender stories that embrace life's large subjects, such as identity seeking, child raising, marriage, illness, education, religion, death, and friendship.

The Simple Living Network
http://www.simpleliving.net

This Web site provides tools and examples for those who are serious about learning to live a more conscious, simple, healthy, and restorative lifestyle.

Simply Living: The Journal of Voluntary Simplicity
(800) 318–5725
www.simpleliving.com

A quarterly publication that inspires and supports people to simplify their lives. Includes first-hand stories, articles, and networking opportunities.

Take Yourself to the Top by Laura Berman Fortgang (New York: Warner Books, 1998)

A career guide written by a talented no-nonsense coach who offers a fresh perspective on success.

LIFE ACCESSORIES

The only outcome is the quality of the day.

ALAN CLEMENTS

After returning from an extremely busy week in London I had a lot of catching up to do. I needed to respond to lots of e-mail, finish writing a column, and read through a stack of mail. I was feeling a bit overwhelmed and as I prepared to get down to business, I decided to put on the soundtrack from the movie *Shine* while I worked in my office. This particular CD was one I had listened to often when I needed a dose of inspiration while writing my first book.

As soon as I began listening to the music, I was struck by how quickly my mood shifted. I went from feeling overwhelmed to feeling overjoyed within seconds. The familiar music brought me right back to a time when I felt energetic and inspired.

As I listened to the CD, I thought about how powerful a mood changer music could be. And I wondered why I hadn't indulged in this pleasure more often while working.

Music is a great example of a life accessory—the simple (and often inexpensive) things that add to the quality of our lives. Much like jewelry or a great tie can enhance an outfit, life accessories are those things that enhance our daily lives by stimulating our senses in positive ways. As a matter of fact, our senses play a key role in identifying these types of accessories.

How might you use life accessories to engage your senses and add richness to your everyday experiences? For example, you might decide to drink tea out of an antique teacup rather than a plain old mug to enhance your visual experience. Or you might use incense or essential oils to add a calming effect to your home or office by engaging your sense of smell. Adding a pet to your home can be an amazing life accessory that enhances your sense of touch, sight, and sound and also provides a great source of love and companionship! Other life accessories may include:

Houseplants or an herb garden

An inspiring or beautiful piece of art hanging on your office wall

Aromatherapy candles

Full-spectrum light bulbs that lift your mood

Listening to a football or baseball game while working

Lighting a fire in the fireplace while cooking a meal

Slipping into warm cozy socks while working at your desk

Fresh flowers

A bubbling fountain

A heating pad to warm your favorite chair or your bed

Great-smelling hair products

Homemade soup simmering on the stove

Hot or cold water dispenser in your office

Your favorite tea

A bird bath or bird feeder outside a window

A sachet in your car or bureau drawers

Heated car seats

It's so easy to get caught up in all there is to do that we forget about these simple pleasures. So, as you start your week, stop for a moment and consider your favorite life accessories. What can you add to your day that will enhance the atmosphere or mood of *your* life?

TAKE ACTION CHALLENGE

As you take some time to consider your life accessories, think about what you love to look at, listen to, taste, smell, and feel. Make a list of at least five examples and use a few this week. When you do, take special notice of the impact it has on your mood and your work.

My five favorite life accessories are:

1. _____

2. _____

3. _____

4. _____

5. _____

RESOURCES

Aura Cacia Aromatherapy

www.auracacia.com

Founded in 1984 in the Trinity Mountains of north-central California, Aura Cacia is a leading manufacturer of 100-percent pure and natural essential oils and quality aromatherapy products.

CHAMPA INCENSE

Blue Pearl
P.O. Box 5127A
Gainesville, FL 32602
www.BluePearlWorld.com

Write for information and a free catalog.

Aromatherapy: An Illustrated Guide by Clare Walters (Boston: Element Books, Inc., 1998)

Beautifully illustrated book that presents an authoritative introduction to the origins and therapeutic powers of aromatherapy. Includes advice on treating ailments and a resource list.

RELAXING MUSIC

David Arkenstone: *Citizen of Time* and *Island*

Enya: *Shepherd Moons* and *Watermark*

Kenny G: *Breathless* and *The Moment*

Loreena McKennit: *Book of Secrets* and *The Mask and the Mirror*

Yanni: *Dare to Dream* and *Devotion: The Best of Yanni*

Van Sickle: *Mother Divine*

Steven Halpern

www.peacethroughmusic.com

THE POWER OF LOVE

Love is a sacred reserve of energy; it is like the blood of spiritual evolution.

PIERRE TEILHARD DE CHARDIN

ove is the divine force that connects us all. Much like electricity, love is the energy that runs through each of us. We share this energy of love in many ways. For example, reaching out to hold a hand or touch a shoulder passes the energy of love through your touch. Speaking kindly to another passes the energy of love through your words. The deliberate use of this force, this energy, produces predictable, powerful results—people feel your love and are healed.

Four years ago I had a direct experience of how the power of love can heal even the most challenging situations. On a warm summer day my friend Max and I were driving to a local supermarket to pick up food for lunch. Traveling down our favorite beach road, we came upon a young man backing out of a driveway. As I stopped to let him out, I was surprised to see that he continued moving backward until he hit my car. Because he gently tapped the bumper, I thought nothing of it until he stepped out and informed me that *I* had hit him. With that, he went back to his car and proceeded to beep his horn until neighbors came to the scene.

I stood by my car in a state of shock as I heard him request an ambulance for his "injured neck." Had Max not been there as a witness, this amazing act of injustice would have made me question whether or not I really *had* hit him. In the next few months I wound up at the center of a lawsuit — I was being sued for causing pain and suffering as well as injuries that resulted in medical expenses.

Here's where the power of love comes in. I was angry. I felt betrayed, and I wanted to hurt this young man. Actually I wanted to kill him, but instead I tried something different. I sent him love. I asked God to send this young man whatever he needed so that he would not need to get it from me in this unlawful way. After all, I figured that if he went to this extreme to get money and attention, then he must have needed it pretty badly. For two months, every day, I imagined him surrounded by love, getting all of his needs met.

Now, believe me, I'm not a saint. And I am not for one minute suggesting that sending love is easy in the face of injustice or betrayal. I am suggesting, however, that for those circumstances that are beyond our control, sending love can be a powerful healing act. As I sent this man love, I noticed something miraculous — I felt better. I relaxed about the situation and was able to let it go.

My friend Barbara learned about the power of love from her niece. Barbara, a single woman in her late fifties, offered to share her small two-bedroom apartment with her sister Carol and her five-year-old daughter, Erica, for a month while they waited for a new home. Used to living alone, Barbara said that she felt nervous about the arrangement, yet she wanted to help her sister out.

During the first two weeks of living together, Barbara thought she'd go crazy. Sharing her personal space with a noisy child caused her so much stress that she eventually came down with the flu. One afternoon, while lying on the couch, Erica came to sit near her. Gently placing her hand on Barbara's forehead, she whispered into her ear, "Don't worry, Aunt Barbara, everything will be okay. I'll take good care of you." In that moment

Barbara's eyes filled with tears. As she looked at her niece, she felt the power of love melt her heart.

Is there someone in your life who needs your love? Your short-fused boss or nosy next door neighbor? Perhaps the grouchy bus driver or your husband's bitter ex-wife? Think of how sending your love to the people you least want to can be a powerful form of healing.

One day after sending love to the man who hit my car, I received a phone call from the police, telling me that a mysterious witness had appeared and the case had been dropped. I can still remember standing with the phone in my hand long after I finished the call. I was shocked. In that moment I understood the power of love. Stronger than anger, hatred, or revenge, love is a powerful force that heals everyone involved. This experience taught me that sending love is also an amazing act of extreme self-care. Because of this experience, I've made the act of sending love my "default button" in any situation. You can too—start today. Is there someone who needs your love?

TAKE ACTION CHALLENGE

Each day we have an opportunity to send messages of love. There are the very direct messages like the "I love you" that we might say to family members. And there are the more subtle messages, like smiling at a stranger or offering a helping hand to a friend in need. This week you get to deliberately send these messages.

Imagine that each morning you are given a pocketful of love to share with others throughout the day (a very *large* pocket). Your mission this week is to empty this pocket daily. You might decide to simply say, "I love you" to someone close (it's usually the people closest to us that need to hear it the most). Or you may reach out to a coworker who drives you crazy and offer to help that person with a project. Maybe you decide to bite your tongue in the middle of an argument and instead offer a kind word or admit you were wrong. Regardless of the situation, stop right now and choose someone. Then pick up the phone and tell that person. Or sit quietly and imagine your energy of love reaching out. As you empty your pocket of love, notice how good it makes you feel too!

The people who most need my love are:

_____

The way I will share this love is by:

_____

RESOURCES

The Post Card Fairy Network
www.postcardfairy.cjb.net

What started out as a spur-of-the-moment posting on the SARK message board has grown into a network of people who send postcards (some of them handmade) to people all over the globe to remind each other that we are all connected. You can join the network for free.

A Return to Love by Marianne Williamson (New York: HarperCollins, 1996)

Reflections on the principles of a Course in Miracles.

Love by Leo Buscaglia (New York: Fawcett Books, September 1996)

Hallmark
www.hallmark.com

You can use the Web site to search for a store near you, to send an online e-card, and so much more!

Blue Mountain Cards
www.bluemountain.com

Send cards for all occasions for free; most have action and music too!

MENTAL SELF-CARE

*I will not let anyone walk through my mind
with their dirty feet.*

MAHATMA GANDHI

By now many of us probably realize the importance of removing the clutter and energy drains from our lives, to prevent us from feeling exhausted and overwhelmed. What you may not realize is that this concept also pertains to your mind.

What you put into your mind through your eyes and your ears (radio, television, newspapers, books, conversations, and so on.) has an amazing impact on your well-being. Several years ago, while attending a workshop, I learned about a research project that was being conducted by a physicist to determine the impact of visual images on the human body. Results showed that our immune system is directly impacted by what we see. For example, when a control group was asked to view one hour of the movie *The Omen*, researchers discovered that the viewer's immune systems were suppressed for thirty days!

It seems that what we hear and feel may also affect our immune system. For example, consider the relationships in your life. Are there people in your life who constantly say things that drain your energy or make you angry? Did you know that these feelings might actually weaken your immune system? Likewise, if there are people who make you feel loved, these feelings might help strengthen your immune system. Consider the following study conducted by the Institute of HeartMath, a California-based nonprofit organization that develops programs aimed at helping people to reduce stress and increase productivity.

The folks at HeartMath took a group of people and measured their base-line levels of IgA, the antibody that intercepts invading germs and pathogens. They asked the study subjects to spend five minutes thinking about something that made them angry. After five minutes they tested the subjects' IgA levels and found that they had increased. One hour later they tested the group again and discovered that IgA levels had dropped to less than half of their base-line reading. Not only that, the researchers found that the subjects' IgA levels were still below the base-line readings *six hours* after recalling the angry episodes.

The same group was tested once more, this time after being asked to recall an experience that made them feel cared for. Once a base line of IgA levels was taken, the participants spent five minutes thinking about an event that allowed them to experience a feeling of sincere caring. Researchers found that the subjects' IgA levels had risen slightly higher than they had in response to the feelings of anger. After one hour the levels had returned to normal. But over the next six hours the IgA levels slowly increased beyond the base-line levels.

What does this study say about the impact of relationships on your health? Perhaps nothing definitive, but you might want to consider whether or not the people in your life are treating you in ways that make you feel loved or angry and stressed out.

Knowing that what you see, hear, and feel impacts your health makes you more conscious of your mental self-care. Imagine what happens when you read a violent story in the newspaper, or hear about a tragedy on the evening news every day! Not only is your body impacted in a negative way, but I'm sure you've felt the emotional and spiritual impact as well. Have you ever noticed your mood shifting after watching a bad television show or after hearing about a crime-related story?

Think of your mind as a large room with limited space. Instead of taking information in at random, remember that everything has an impact. Choose wisely. If you find yourself at a movie that suddenly turns violent or offensive, leave and ask for your money back (theaters usually give refunds). Or, when reading a book that no longer holds your interest, don't push your way through to the end filling your mind with worthless information; stop where you are and let it go. As you carefully choose what goes into your mind, watch what happens to your life. After all, it's what we hold in our mind that shows up in our lives when we're not looking.

TAKE ACTION CHALLENGE

During this week, practice mental self-care. Do your body, mind, and soul a favor and replace the negative television programs, radio shows, or conversations that bring you down with something uplifting and positive. Turn off the nonsense on TV and read a good book instead. Or forget the radio talk show on the way to work and listen to some relaxing music. There's a good chance that these new behaviors will feel uncomfortable at first, but if you hang on through the discomfort, you'll find peace and serenity (as well as improved health) waiting on the other side!

RESOURCES

Heartmath Solution by Doc Lew Childre, Howard Martin, and Donna Beech (New York: HarperCollins, 1999)
www.heartmath.com

The Heartmath Institute offers programs that help to reduce stress and improve personal effectiveness.

Utne Reader Magazine
Utne Reader Subscriber Service
P.O. Box 7460
Red Oak, IA 51591-0460
(800) 736–UTNE
www.utne.com

Utne Reader reprints the best articles from over 2,000 alternative media sources, bringing you the latest ideas and trends emerging in our culture. Utne's "Web Watch Daily" includes hot topics and headline news from across the world.

Hope Magazine
Hope Subscriptions
P.O. Box 160
Brooklin, ME 04616
(800) 273–7447

A great read, this magazine offers stories of hope and inspiration. Subscription is $24.95 for one year.

New Age Magazine
42 Water Street
Watertown, MA 02172
(617) 926–0200

New Age reports on leading-edge ideas in the areas of health, natural living, self-improvement, psychology, publishing, and music.

PEOPLE AND PRIORITIES

Do everything in connection.

ED SHEA

As my busy travel season starts to wind down, I've been using my morning journal-writing time to reconsider my priorities for the next year. I am enormously grateful for all that has occurred in my life over the last year. The success of my first book and the opportunity to travel around the country meeting wonderful people has been a dream come true. I've worked hard, and the rewards have been worth it.

One of the greatest gifts my busy travel schedule has given me is a keen awareness of what really matters. There's something about being away from home and spending less time with loved ones that puts things into perspective.

Although a published book and a public life appear to be attractive accomplishments, they pale in comparison to the deep, lasting connections I share with family and friends. It's taken a year of being away and the fulfillment of a dream to really understand this on a deep level.

When we come to the end of our lives, it's not the career success, accomplishments, or the size of our bank accounts that will matter. Instead, it will be the people we've loved and who have loved us that will make our lives (and hearts) feel full. It's so easy to take our important relationships for granted. We get wrapped up in our busy lives, and the first people to pay the price are those closest to us—partner, family, children, friends. Life's responsibilities get in the way, and we find ourselves making excuses to loved ones in the hopes that they'll understand (and they usually do, for a while).

Making your relationships a higher priority might mean saying no to your boss when she asks you to work late, so you can have dinner with your family. Sometimes the choices are even more challenging, like agreeing to pass on a great job opportunity so you won't need to relocate your family. When we make the people in our lives more of a priority, we eventually realize that the rewards are well worth the sacrifices. Our careers may be important, but our connection with loved ones lasts a lifetime.

As I consider my plans for the next year, I've decided to make my relationships a higher priority. To do this, I'll need to say no to things that I'd really like to do. I'll be challenged to face my fear of losing ground by taking time away from professional activities. For example, I may need to give up a big speaking engagement in order to celebrate a special event with my family or friends. Or I might have to delay a writing deadline to reduce my stress level so that I'm more pleasant to be around.

In addition to changing plans, I'll need to invest my time and energy in learning to relate on a deeper, more intimate level. How about you? Are you willing to invest more deeply in the relationships that matter most? Is there someone who needs your care and attention? Someone you've been taking for granted? What about the new skills *you'll* need to learn in order to deepen your relationships? Are you able to listen without judgment, be honest with how you feel, and confront a difficult issue directly instead of using silence as a barrier to intimacy?

Don't let a busy day rob you of what really counts as success at the end of a long, full life. Reconsider your priorities now and give yourself (and others) the gift of your love and attention.

TAKE ACTION CHALLENGE

As you finish this chapter, take a few moments to consider the following:

1. Who are the people in your life that matter most?

2. What kind of attention or care do these relationships need?

3. What new skill do you need to acquire in order to invest more deeply in these relationships?

4. What will you *do* differently to insure that your relationships get the attention they deserve?

RESOURCES

Getting the Love You Want: A Guide for Couples by Harville Hendrix, Ph.D. (New York: HarperPerennial Library, 1990)

A terrific practical guide to resolving problems, using sixteen exercises to enhance communication, stop self-defeating behavior, and achieve mutual emotional satisfaction.

Relationship Rescue by Phillip C. McGraw (New York: Hyperion, 2000)

A seven-step strategy for reconnecting with your partner. McGraw has distilled his more than two decades of counseling experience into a seven-step strategy he calls Relationship Rescue.

GREAT GIFT GIVING

We make a living by what we get, but we make a life by
what we give.

WINSTON CHURCHILL

I
n the spirit of honoring relationships and the holiday season, I've decided to use this chapter to share five of my favorite holiday gift ideas. These suggestions are designed to inspire you to be more creative with your gift giving this year while deepening your connection to loved ones.

1. *Write a love letter (or poem) to your partner.* How many times have you struggled to find the perfect gift for your significant other, only to wind up settling for something mediocre? Well, if you've ever received a love letter, you know how very special this gift can be (for both men and women!). Take some time to put your feelings down on beautiful paper. Once you've completed the letter or poem, be sure to wrap it in a gift box. If you're concerned about your writing ability, then make it easy. For example, you could create a top-ten list that says: The Top Ten Reasons Why I Love You Are. . . .

2. *Write a book for someone you love.* This is actually much easier than it sounds and can be a great creative project for those of you who long to publish a book. Think of it as a practice run. Choose someone special (spouse, partner, family member, or friend), purchase

a small, beautiful journal, and over the next month or so write one page a day.

I did this for my husband Michael one year. Each day I wrote a letter to him reflecting on something that I admired, loved, or respected. There were some days when I felt inspired to write more than a page. By the time Christmas arrived, I had filled a small book, and this gift meant more to him than anything else I'd ever given him.

3. *Plan a surprise event.* Choose someone special and plan an event that you know the gift receiver would really love. Pick a date, create a mysterious invitation, and wrap it up.

One of my clients did this for his wife. He found a romantic inn, scheduled a baby-sitter, and planned a weekend getaway in early January. Because this gift was a surprise, his wife got to enjoy an extended holiday season and get an unexpected rest.

4. *Give a gift of your time and energy.* Think about the kind of service or support that the people in your life could most benefit from receiving, and offer that as a gift. For example, do you have a brother or sister who could use a weekend away while you watch the children or help with lining up baby-sitters? Or what about a friend who needs help organizing or setting up a bookkeeping system? Design a fun gift certificate (with an actual date of service) and wrap it in a box.

5. *Lift a burden.* Purchase a gift certificate for a service that you know someone could really use. For example, you might give a busy entrepreneur the gift of a personal chef for a month. Or why not offer lawn-care services to a friend with a bad back? How about pooling your resources with other family members and give a gift of several weeks or months of housekeeping to a busy mom (by the way, this is the #1 desire of women in my audiences who are raising children).

Who knows, by using one of these gift ideas, you might find yourself falling in love with holiday shopping all over again.

TAKE ACTION CHALLENGE

Pick one idea from the above list and make it fun. The earlier you get started, the more meaningful the gift will be to you and the lucky recipient.

The people I'd like to give a special gift to are:

1. _____

2. _____

3. _____

The gift I will give them is:

1. _____

2. _____

3. _____

RESOURCES

Illuminations
1995 South McDowell Blvd.
Petaluma, CA 94954
www.illuminations.com

A wonderful place to buy beautiful candles and gifts.

Flooz Money for Great On-Line Gifts
www.flooz.com

Flooz is the on-line gift currency you can send by e-mail. Recipients spend Flooz just like money at the on-line store of their choice.

www.MrsBeasley.com

This Web site offers a variety of wonderful gifts that include cookies, cakes, and more.

THE "THANK YOU" GAME

If the only prayer you say in your life is "thank you,"
that would suffice.

MEISTER ECKHART

This week I'd like to invite you to play a game. This game is inspired by my father, who, for as long as I can remember, has loved to surprise people with gifts of gratitude. For example, he's been known to deliver fruit baskets to the local nursing homes and miniature Christmas trees to his elderly clients. And one day he even chased a rubbish truck down the street in order to give the attendants money to buy themselves breakfast. My dad is a very special man.

The object of this week's game—let's call it the Thank You game—is to find a creative and inexpensive way to thank or acknowledge those people in your life who often get overlooked. For example, you might acknowledge or appreciate those people who provide you with everyday services. Have some fun! For example you might do something like:

1. Bring a box of chocolate-chip cookies to your local post office or copy shop and thank the employees for their hard work throughout the year. Believe me, this means a lot!

2. Dial 411 and thank the operator for providing information all year long (don't be surprised if there's a period of stunned silence).

3. Send a thank-you card to someone who would least expect it, like your landscaper, auto mechanic, doctor, or lawyer.

4. Bring an apple pie to the staff of a local shelter, Goodwill or Salvation Army office to thank them for *their* dedication to a cause.

5. Leave a larger-than-normal tip for your local wait person who serves you coffee or breakfast (you could even invite that person to have breakfast with you!).

The idea is to unleash your creative spirit and experience the joy of thanking others. As you play the Thank You game, you'll probably discover what my dad learned many years ago: saying thank you and giving to others feels so good that you'll want to do it all year long.

TAKE ACTION CHALLENGE

Stop for a moment and browse through your address book, Rolodex, or database program and identify the people who help make your life easier. Then make a list of these people and set out this week to thank one special person a day. It might be a massage therapist, post-officer clerk, doctor, lawyer, accountant, copy-shop proprietor, or financial planner.

The seven people I'd like to thank are:

1. _____

2. _____

3. _____

4. _____

5. _____

6. _____

7. _____

RESOURCES

Fairytale Brownies
(800) 324–7982
www.fairytalebrownies.com

Scrumptious brownies baked from scratch. They're inexpensive, beautifully wrapped, and wonderful!

Bloomin' Flower Cards
2510 North 47th St., Studio E
Boulder, CO 80301
(800) 894–9185
www.bloomin.com

A great resource for inexpensive gift cards that, when planted, grow all kinds of plants or flowers.

Marliese Designs
(508) 520–4839

Marliese is an artist who makes gorgeous hand-painted affirmation cards as well as painted clothing and gifts.

THE BENEFITS
OF BOREDOM

Boredom is the gateway to peace.

THOMAS LEONARD

After traveling around the country for long stretches at a time, I was busy running from one meeting to another, using adrenaline as my main source of fuel. I had forgotten that the transition into a slower rhythm could feel a bit uncomfortable. It can feel pretty boring when you start to slow down. Fortunately I know about the benefits of boredom. When I start to feel bored, I know I'm getting close to the peace of mind my soul longs for.

Boredom is the feeling many people first experience when they have time in their schedule with nothing to do, when we have unexpected time on our hands, or when we challenge ourselves to be still so that we can listen to our Wise Self. It's not uncommon to feel uncomfortable, and often this discomfort feels like boredom.

I did a little research on boredom. I asked several friends about their ability to slow down and do nothing. Clearly it's not an easy thing for most people to "do." Many friends said that the minute they had extra time on their hands, they felt compelled to do something. Together we laughed at the kind of things we've done. See if you can identify with any of them. . . .

You know you have a tough time with boredom when:

1. You keep a box of dental floss, nail files, pens, and paper in your car so you have something to do when you hit a traffic jam.

2. You begin cleaning out your purse or wallet when you have extra time before an appointment.

3. You clean the dashboard of your car while waiting in a slow-moving drive-thru line at your local coffee shop.

4. You start dusting the furniture or cleaning out drawers when you finally have a night to yourself.

5. When you have a spare half-hour during the day, you call someone who drains your energy.

6. You start reading the phone book in a hotel room. (This was not my example.)

7. You find yourself engrossed in a story about a three-headed baby while standing in the checkout line at the grocery store.

In an adrenaline-fueled society, learning to do nothing can feel pretty challenging. Too often we fill up our lives with activities, tasks, or busyness to avoid feeling bored. Years of focusing our attention "out there" makes it difficult to take the time and space to look inward and spend time reflecting on our lives. Often what lies beneath the feelings of boredom is fear of the unknown, of facing unmet dreams, or a desire to remain detached from the feelings we've suppressed for years. But, with practice, you'll discover that learning to sit with the feelings of boredom that quickly give way to a deeper reflection of your life eventually leads to a sense of peace and serenity that will fuel you in a whole new way.

I learned about the benefits of boredom from my first coach.

During the time that we worked together he challenged me to master the art of being bored in order to get to the peace of mind on the other side — something I longed for at that time in my life. To do this, I had to create much more space in my life than I felt comfortable with in order to do nothing and learn to sit with myself for a while. For example, I needed to clear my schedule so that I had more nights and weekends free than I was used to so I could simply let my mind wander. I needed to let go of several projects and goals (even some I really wanted) in order to limit my distractions. I had to stop my relentless pursuit of new opportunities and "great ideas" so that I could settle down, be with my own thoughts, identify my true priorities, and connect with a spiritual power that would allow me to accomplish my important goals more effectively.

Learning to be bored is like learning to meditate. As you schedule time for yourself without doing anything (no TV, reading, talking on the phone, and the like), you'll need to hang on through a period of restlessness before you can settle down and experience the benefits. Once you get used to it, you not only learn to relax and reduce stress, you learn much more. You learn to be with your thoughts and enjoy your own company. You learn to develop the self-discipline that serves you in other areas of your life. You learn to be less impulsive, and as a result you make better decisions.

As you begin to practice being bored, you will most likely experience the typical fear-based thoughts that will try to pull you back into "doing." They go something like this:

"Everyone else is getting ahead but me."

"I'm missing out on important opportunities."

"I won't succeed fast enough."

"I'm being irresponsible and/or unproductive."

These thoughts are just your mind telling you lies in the hopes of keeping you busy and disconnected from your true Self. Here's the truth: once you get good at being bored and are able to maintain a reserve of space in your life, you will engage a spiritual power that will draw toward you the best people, opportunities, and resources that will serve you in a much better way. If this sounds a bit far-fetched, don't take my word for it, give boredom a try. Start making space in your life and watch what happens.

TAKE ACTION CHALLENGE

This week become mindful of how you avoid boredom and being with your own thoughts. What do *you* do to fill up your time? As you notice these behaviors, challenge yourself to stop them, breathe, and sit with the discomfort.

Next, consciously make space in your life to practice being still. Look over your calendar and make the necessary changes to free up some time. Consider your goals, projects, and commitments and challenge yourself to let go of some of them in order to free up your time (how about 50 percent of them!). Then sit with the extra space in your life for the next two or three months and experience the process of moving beyond boredom to the peace and serenity waiting on the other side.

The five ways that I avoid boredom are:

1. _____

2. _____

3. _____

4. _____

5. _____

The three goals, projects, or commitments I will let go of are:

1. _____

2. _____

3. _____

RESOURCES

The Art of Doing Nothing by Veronique Vienne and Erica Lennard (New York: Potter, 1998)

Wonderful essays and photographs on the art of breathing, meditating, bathing, listening, waiting, and more.

Stopping: How to Be Still When You Have to Keep Going by David Kundtz (New York: Conari Press, 1998)

This book shows the reader how to stop in any situation to regain a sense of purpose and see the light of grace.

STOP THE MADNESS

The only gift is a portion of thyself.

RALPH WALDO EMERSON

Here we are in the middle of another holiday season. Are you rushing around trying to find the perfect gifts? Have you squeezed in the decorating between a busy work schedule and your daily obligations? And amid all the running around, have you been wondering how the spirit of the holiday season got lost among the chaos?

In this age of consumerism and information overload it's too easy to feel overwhelmed and exhausted. Many of us long to re-capture the spirit of the holiday season, and yet we lack the energy or motivation to do something about it.

You have a choice about the quality of your holiday season. You can continue to rush around like a crazy man or woman, or you can stop right now and make a decision to do something different. To support you in taking a different approach to the holidays, I thought I'd make some suggestions that might help you reclaim the spirit of the season before it's too late.

1. *Forgo gift buying for an evening dinner with friends.* Ask your friends to participate in a new holiday ritual. Instead of exchanging gifts, plan an intimate gathering *after* the holidays. The week between Christmas and the New Year is usually quiet, and most people feel either a sense of relief or a bit let down. It's the perfect time to

get together and enjoy the company of those you love. (Most people are more available then, too.)

2. *Create an intentional memory.* Gather your family or friends together for a night of caroling at a local nursing home. Adopt a soup kitchen, invite a few friends to join you, and spend an afternoon serving others. How about a day of ice skating with the kids or a family sleigh ride? For many of us the true spirit of the holiday season comes from giving and sharing quality time with loved ones. If you put some intention behind these desires, and plan a special event, you'll have a wonderful memory that will last much longer than any gift.

3. *Cut back on the gift buying.* My family started a new tradition several years ago. Instead of buying gifts for each other (a lot of work for fourteen of us!), we decided to put each family member's name into a hat so we could choose one person to buy for. In the past we've done this for the siblings, and we've now added the nieces and nephews. Not only does it make shopping less stressful, it allows the children to receive fewer gifts so that they can appreciate the ones they do get more fully.

4. *Use technology to your advantage.* Buy your gifts on line or from catalogs. Set aside an afternoon, light a fire (or put on holiday music), and search for the best gifts. Then spend half an hour the next morning placing your orders. When you cut out the travel time and shopping-mall lines, and add in the online discounts, you'll save money and have much more time to spend with loved ones.

5. *Engage your senses.* One of the quickest ways to get into a more festive mood is to feed your senses a good dose of holiday cheer. Break out your favorite holiday music and listen to it throughout the day. Light some pine incense or a bayberry candle and let the aroma bring back warm memories.

And finally, sometimes the best way to enjoy the holidays is to give yourself permission to sit this one out. This can be especially important if you are going through a time of transition, grieving a loss, or just experiencing a low mood. It's perfectly fine to let go of expectations and take good care of your soul. The important thing to remember is that *you* are in charge of your holiday experience. If you don't *do* something different, you'll lose one more holiday to the media, malls, and madness!

TAKE ACTION CHALLENGE

Take a moment and identify two things that you'd like to do differently this season. Then, take action to make the changes *today*. Next, add some "holiday accessories" to your life. Listen to your favorite holiday music at work, or go out at lunch and buy a small wreath for your office door (looks festive and smells great too!).

The two things that I'll do differently this year are:

1. _____

2. _____

My favorite holiday accessory is:

_____

RESOURCES

Pickles, Peaches, and Chocolate: Easy, Elegant Gifts from Your Kitchen by Karen Ward (California: C&K Enterprises, 1999)

An assortment of recipes that make wonderful treats for gift giving.

SoapWerks
806 S. Dogwood Dr.
Berea, KY 40403
(877) 985–7877

Bath and bodycare products that are made in small batches using only top-quality vegetable oils, herbs, beeswax, and essential oils. Each product is lovingly wrapped and packaged by hand.

www.naterra.com

This company offers "CandleSong," an aromatherapy candle that plays CD-quality music when lit. A unique conversation piece, it makes a great inexpensive gift that provides a wonderful scent and stress-reliever all in one.

Unplug the Christmas Machine: A Complete Guide to Putting Love and Joy Back into the Season by Jo Robinson and Jean Coppock Staeheli (New York: Quill, 1991)

Unplug the Christmas Machine remains one of the most comprehensive guides to managing Christmas stress and combating commercialism. Jo Robinson and Jean Coppock Staeheli give readers solid advice on how to make their celebrations more spiritual and less materialistic. Although this book is geared toward Christmas, it has information that you might find useful for reducing stress on any other holiday.

SHAKE UP YOUR LIFE

Sanity calms, but madness is more interesting.

JOHN RUSSELL

I'm writing this chapter from the middle of a dismantled office. I'm finally getting to those projects that I've been putting off over the last year, and repainting my office had been top on my list. Over the weekend my phone and fax lines were shut down. My furniture has been covered with plastic and moved to the middle of the room. And my walls were painted an amazing color that looks like a combination of orange and raspberry sherbet.

During this mini project my good friend and colleague Steve Shull, a terrific coach from Los Angeles, called to let us know he was coming into town on business. Well, I never turn down an opportunity to hang out with a dear friend (and a fellow coach), so I invited Steve to stay with us.

Normally I would have thought that having our home in a state of disarray while hosting a house guest would have thrown my life into chaos, but it did something wonderful instead. It shook up the normal routine of my daily life and allowed me to let go and have some fun.

There's something about changing our environment and shaking up our daily routine that's good for the soul. For example, I never would have thought that painting my office a bold, bright new color would unleash a flood of creative inspiration. Once my office was painted, I found myself wanting to completely change the layout of the room. And from there, I started wandering around the house imagining all kinds of new changes that I'd like to make happen. My soul was enjoying the pleasure of creating.

Along with the creative inspiration came the fun. Sharing our home with a friend forced me to shift my normal daily routine. Rather than jump into work first thing in the morning, we'd go out for breakfast. During the day I made a point of focusing on getting the most important priorities handled so that we'd have plenty of time for socializing in the afternoons and evenings.

Shaking up my life paid big dividends. It reminded me of where joy lives—in taking time to express my creative spirit and in the company of those I love. How about you? Could your life use a little shaking up? Are you willing to make a change in your daily routine? When we change the external landscape of our lives, we automatically shift the internal landscape as well. Sometimes this helps us to get even clearer about our true priorities. It did for me.

TAKE ACTION CHALLENGE

Shake up your life a bit this week. Move furniture around. Stop in the middle of your workday and do something fun. Go out on a night on which you usually stay home, and enjoy a spontaneous dinner with a friend. If you're self-employed, sneak out one afternoon and take in a movie. It's the end of the year, why not let the holiday season prompt you to do something a bit out of the ordinary?

The one thing I'll do to shake up my life this week is:

_____

SANE AND SPECIAL

Imagination is the one weapon in the war against reality.

JULES DE GAULTIER

During this final week before the holidays and potential madness I'd like to offer a few simple things you can do to help make this week sane and special.

1. *Smile more*—even when you're feeling overwhelmed or at your wit's end, you can trick your body into a state of joy by holding a smile on your face for at least thirty seconds. Try it right now.

2. One evening this week pack the family (or friends) in the car, go for a drive, and *enjoy the lights and decorations in your neighborhood*. Make sure to play holiday music at the same time. This kind of event makes for a great memory. Many years later I still remember my seventy-five-year-old grandmother squealing with delight as my sisters and I took her around town so that she could enjoy the lights.

3. When everyone's gone to bed, *sit quietly by the fire or the Christmas tree* and enjoy five minutes of silence (without putting any toys together).

4. *Help a parent.* Giving to others always makes the holidays special. While visiting with my cousin and fellow coach Sharon Day

(who is an amazing mom), she talked about how parents often get overlooked when it comes time for appreciation and recognition. Well, the holidays are the perfect time to acknowledge the parents in your life who have chosen to take on the most sacred career of all—raising children. This week send a mom or dad a special card, e-mail, or voice mail thanking them for all they do (you might even offer to help with last-minute cooking or gift wrapping too!)

5. *Practice "traffic singing."* My husband Michael and I were out shopping one day when we came upon a traffic singer. At one point, while stopped at a red light, Michael started laughing out loud and asked me to look in the rearview mirror. Behind us was a well-dressed man dancing in his seat and singing at the top of his lungs. Well, Michael and I enjoyed his joy so much that I wanted to get out and thank him for adding to the quality of our day. Start singing in traffic and add a little joy to those around you.

Whether you take one of the suggestions above, or practice some of your own, I do wish each and every one of you a warm and memorable holiday.

TAKE ACTION CHALLENGE

A very simple action this week:

Breathe . . .

THE POWER OF PRAYER

The soul grows well when giving and receiving love. Love is,
after all, a verb, an action word, not a noun.

JOAN BORYSENKO

For the past fifty-one weeks I have focused these chapters on self-care strategies in an effort to support you in improving the quality of your life. I've done this for a very important reason: experience has taught me that when we care more deeply for ourselves, we cannot help but care more deeply for others and for this planet that we share together.

As my life unfolds, I feel an enormous amount of gratitude. It's in the spirit of this gratitude that I feel a responsibility to contribute to the world in even greater ways. And as you've begun to reclaim a sense of purpose and meaning in your life by practicing these strategies, I'm sure you've experienced a similar opening of your heart.

As we come to the end of one amazing year and stand on the threshold of another, it's a perfect time to consider how you might share your good fortune. How will you bring what you've learned from these pages into the world in order to improve the quality of life for others? What gifts would you like to share with those in need?

Service is the highest form of spiritual engagement. In our final week together I'd like to invite you to create a new daily ritual of service that will challenge you to open your heart to others on a regular basis. There are several things you can do. For example, you might choose one way to help someone in need each day like delivering food to an elderly neighbor or offering your support to a frustrated coworker. You might make a daily visit to the Hunger Site *(www.thehungersite.com)*, a place where visitors can donate free food to the hungry at no cost once a day simply through the click of a button. The Hunger Site's sponsors pay for these donations, distributed by the United Nations World Food Program.

An act of daily service can be as simple as lending an ear to someone in need or letting a stranger into traffic on a busy street. The point is to look for an opportunity to serve at least one person every day.

In addition to looking for ways to be of service every day, you can choose to offer your time, attention, or resources in a variety of ways. One of my favorite rituals of service has to do with the power of prayer. I keep a special candle in my office, and when a friend, family member, client, or member of my on-line community, is in need, I light the candle and pray for a successful resolution to the person's problem or challenge. I believe strongly in the power of prayer to create miracles in our lives. I've learned firsthand that when a group of people join forces by putting their minds and hearts together in a positive, powerful direction, miracles happen. Let me share a story that demonstrates what I mean.

Several years ago my brother's newborn daughter became seriously ill. She contracted an unusual respiratory virus and ended up in the hospital fighting for her life. I felt frightened for my brother and sister-in-law and was desperate to do something to help.

During this time I was reading Larry Dossey's book, *Healing Words*, about research that was being conducted to study the efficacy of prayer. Dossey had found more than 130 scientific studies in the general area of healing that included prayer. More than half of these experiments strongly indicated that prayer worked. Although I didn't know it at the time, I was about to conduct an experiment of my own.

On the day my niece became critically ill, I sent an e-mail to everyone I knew asking them to stop what they were doing, light a candle, and pray that my niece be healed immediately. I was scared and included anyone and everyone I could think of in this request for help. Once the message was sent, I quickly lit a candle and began praying myself.

I was comforted by the e-mails I received letting me know that people were praying and holding healing intentions (probably fifty people altogether). That evening, in the middle of the night, my niece had what doctors called "a miraculous recovery." They were shocked to discover that her condition went from critical to stable in a matter of a few short hours.

Was it prayer that healed her? I'll never know for sure, but that experience taught me something. It taught me to place my bets on the power of the Divine to work through people. I learned that when people share an intention based in love, miracles occur.

What does this story have to do with the ending of this book? As you enter into the next year of your life, along with creating your own daily ritual of service in the Take Action Challenge below, I'd like to invite you to join me in a ritual to celebrate the completion of your work.

When you've reached the end of this book, light a candle, sit quietly, and imagine a world where each human being is fed, free, and fearless. See the world calmly and peacefully moving into a Golden Age where wisdom and love become a powerful force for change. It doesn't matter whether or not you believe in the power of prayer, hold the intention anyway. You never know, there just may be a miracle waiting for us all. . . .

TAKE ACTION CHALLENGE

This week I invite you to share your love, knowledge, money, time, attention, or whatever gifts you have to offer with someone in need. Create your own daily ritual of service and put it into practice. You might remind yourself of your daily gift of service by putting a check mark in your calendar at the end of every day. Or start your day with a morning ritual by simply asking yourself, "How can I serve one person today?" and writing the answer in your journal.

Share what you've learned from these pages with those who will benefit from your wisdom and experience. Whether you send a donation to a worthy cause, donate blood, or offer to help a coworker solve a problem, give yourself an opportunity to experience the power of opening your heart in service to others.

The people I'd most like to serve are:

_____

The way I can contribute is:

_____

The first action I'll take to put a new service ritual in place is:

_____

RESOURCES

Habitat for Humanity International
121 Habitat St.
Americus, GA 31709
(912) 924–6935
www.habitat.org

Welcomes volunteers from all faiths to join together to build decent, affordable housing. Houses are sold with no profit made.

National Hospice Organization (NHO)
1901 North Moore Street,
Suite 901
Arlington, VA 22209
(703) 243–5900
www.nho.org

Hospice care is a compassionate method of caring for terminally ill people. You can search their Web site database to find a center in your area.

The Courage to Give by Jackie Waldman with Janis Leibs Dworkis (New York: Conari Press, 1999)

Poignant and uplifting stories of people who triumphed over tragedy and made a difference in the world. From Millard Fuller, the founder of Habitat for Humanity, to Patch Adams, these courageous individuals have risen phoenixlike, consciously deciding to devote their lives to others. The book also identifies organizations dedicated to the issues it raises, so that readers can learn more and lend support.

http://www.Volunteermatch.org

VolunteerMatch utilizes the power of the Internet to help individuals nationwide find volunteer opportunities posted by local nonprofit and public-sector organizations.

Volunteers of America
National Office
110 South Union Street
Alexandria, Virginia 22314
(800) 899–0089
www.voa.org

A nonprofit organization that offers over 160 programs to assist children, youth, the elderly, families in crisis, the homeless, people with disabilities or mental illness, and ex-convicts returning to society.

The Voice of Hope: Conversations with Burma's Nobel laureate Aung San Suu Kyi by Alan Clements, (New York: Seven Stories Press, 1998)

A moving and eye-opening dialogue that demonstrates the power of love, courage, and forgiveness in Burma's nationwide nonviolent "revolution of the spirit" for freedom.

www.WorldDharma.com

A community of seekers exploring the link between our inner journey and engagement with the outer world through love, creativity, and service.

You can subscribe to the community's e-newsletter broadcast — *Spirit In Action: A Guide to Liberation Through Living* — by visiting their Web site.

Cheryl Richardson was the first president of the International Coach Federation and received one of the first Master Certified Coach credentials issued in the United States. She speaks professionally to audiences throughout the United States and Europe, and is the host and co-executive producer of "The Life Makeover Project" series on the Oxygen network. She lives in Massachusetts.